FEARLESS MARKETING
Your 8-Figure Business Blueprint

FEARLESS MARKETING:
Your 8-Figure Business Blueprint

Marketing doesn't have to be a mystery

ISBN-13: 978-1727811643

ISBN-10: 172781164X

Published By ICK com. llc Publishing House©
Edited By ICK Publishing & Cat Schmidt Lewis
Cover Design and Book Design By ICK Publishing©

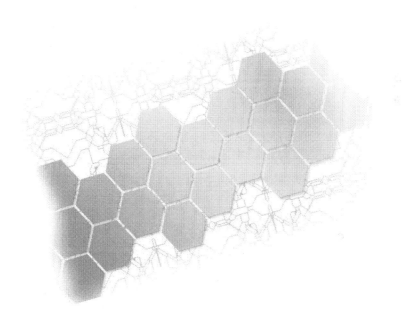

Your 8-Figure Business Blueprint

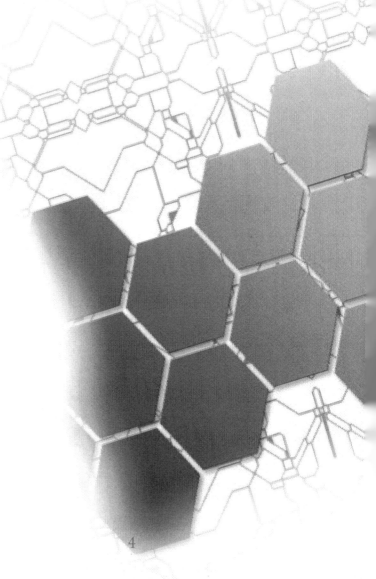

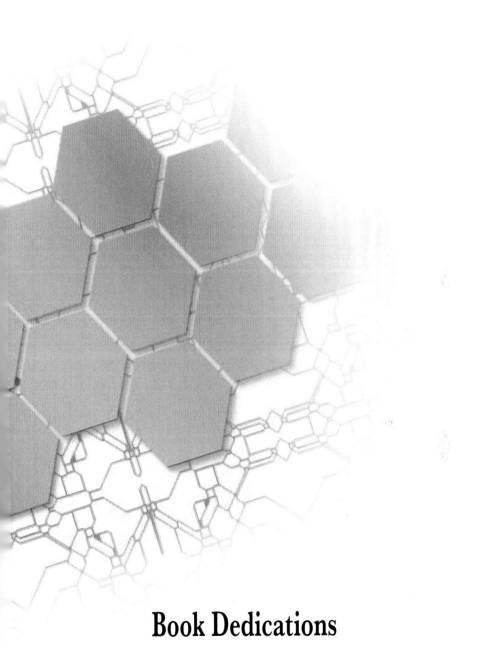

Book Dedications

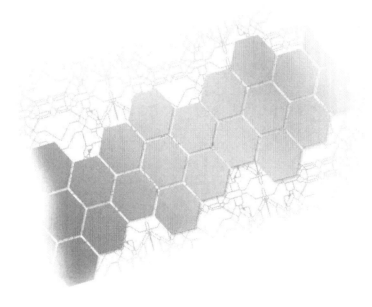

Book Dedications

This book is dedicated to the amazing women in my life who have supported me through the process of growing and writing this book.

Specifically, I'd like to thank Irene Pro, Cat Schmidt Lewis, Heather Fein, ZofiaRenea Morales, Leigh Scheidell, Leslie Flowers, and everyone who read, edited, and reviewed this book.

~Haley lynn Gray

Your 8-Figure Business Blueprint

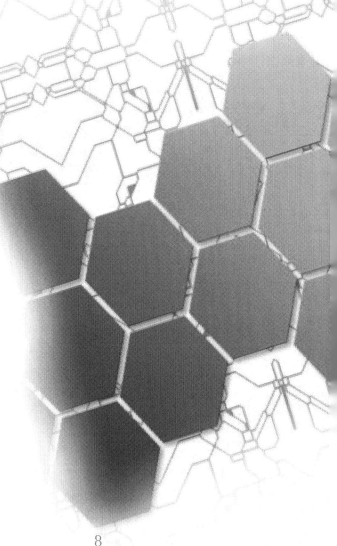

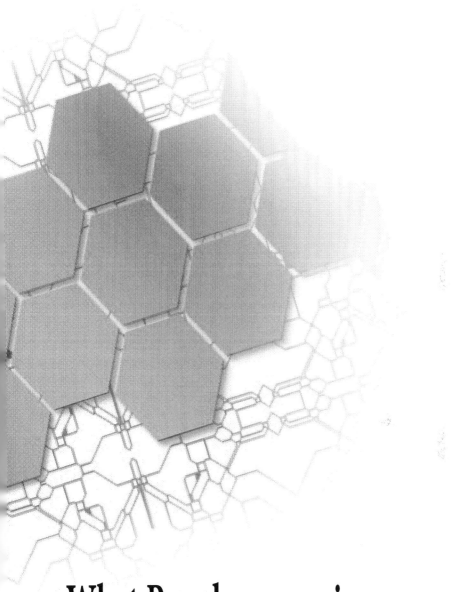

What People are saying...

What People are saying...

From branding to figuring out your target customer, this book is a great tool that helped me to take my marketing fears away. The concepts are divided clearly, allowing me to review and implement them one at a time removing that overwhelming feeling! ~ **Kim Sloan**

No matter where you are in your entrepreneurial journey, the information in this book can help ensure your foundational pieces are properly in place so you are able to scale appropriately as you grow. Get this part wrong and you will be scrambling to adjust at every turn.

Marketing is one of the key components to a successful business. "Fearless Marketing: Your 8-Figure Business Blueprint" covers all the steps involved from $0 sales through a couple of stages all the way to 8 figures. You will learn to reverse engineer your goals based upon the end results you wish to achieve. Step-by-step processes are laid out for achieving your business dreams when following this blueprint.

Save yourself the mistakes made by others which can be avoided by establishing these processes to attain your end goal. I highly recommend this book before you get started or if you feel you may be stuck in a rut which is taking you nowhere fast.

~ **Leigh Scheidell, Video Creative**

Haley's book offers solid and practical advice for every entrepreneur whether a beginner or million dollar success story. Her easy to follow, tried and true information is a must for everyone to endeavor to follow.

~**Karen A. Thomas, Etiquette Expert**

This is my new business bible! I wish I would have had this when I started my business. Haley has created an easily digestible and organized plan for success. My business is no longer dying, its thriving.

~**April Scotece**

What People are saying...

"I was concerned that I would not gain much new insight, but after working with Haley, I got a few new ideas on marketing options to look into.

Haley is very engaged in her conversation with you and you can hear the wheels spinning when she thinks through how to uniquely help your business. She is masterful when it comes to giving incite to marketing efforts and how to navigate the social media tangled web.

If you work with Haley, you will not be disappointed. She does provide one on one services at a reasonable rate but also provides a wealth of knowledge through her books, blogs and free online resources. Thanks Haley!"

~Jennie K.

"Before working with Haley, my group was literally gathering dust and I just didn't want to spend ages googling for advice or spend money on yet another online course.

Haley is just really hands on with practical and tested advice and knows how it works. Plus I really enjoy her personality, so it was a joy talking with her.

If you want someone who is kind, but also down to earth and business savvy, then you need Haley. She is a business machine!"

~Christine H

"Haley is an amazingly dynamic force. She always has several irons in the fire and manages them all with great skill. When Haley commits herself to a task, you can be sure that it will be completed well."

~Samantha Herring

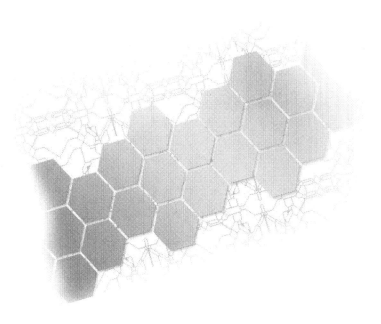

Content

Your 8-Figure Business Blueprint

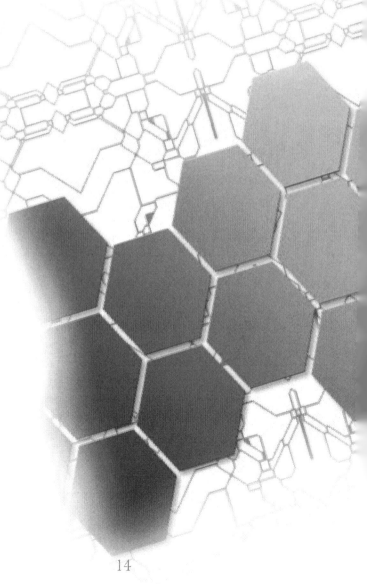

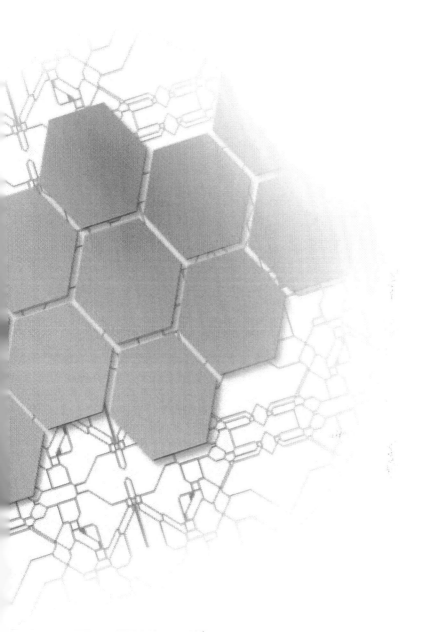

Foreword

"The mighty poles that suspend the tent are each of the chapters in this book; all eighteen of them! They all have equal weight and value to the structure."

Foreword

Let's not waste your time. Before you begin reading this book, check in to see if you match the two bullet points below. If you do, proceed hungrily, for you are in for a real feast.

- If you are a person who not only wants things yet is also willing to do what it takes to achieve them with some consistency and predictability, this book is for you. You do not give up (that's why you are reading this!).

- If you are still confused and confounded about this nebulous thing called marketing, and you've invested time and revenue with little to show for it, this book is for you. You want to Solve this problem once and for all!

I first met Haley Lynn Gray at a small business event I hosted in 2016. She was very quiet and struck me as an observer; objective and responsive. My jaw dropped when soon after that meeting I learned she grew a Facebook group to some 60,000 entrepreneurs in under two years! I wanted to know HOW she did it in such short order. That was two years ago. As this book is released, it's another jaw dropping moment for me as I saw the way Haley Lynn Gray crafted this book for you; those who match the bullet points above.

Consider for a moment, MARKETING to be a large big top circus tent, hoisted twenty to sixty feet (at center) above the ground, suspended on lots of anchored steel poles.

The mighty poles that suspend the tent are each of the chapters in this book; all eighteen of them! They all have equal weight and value to the structure.

If you attempt to erect the tent with less than all eighteen, the foundation is compromised and the tent will be out of integrity for sure.

Like me, you may be wondering how truly rare it would be to have one person explain everything about the value of each pole and the overarching concept of Marketing, in a simple, step by step checklist fashion! We are already Willing to do what it takes.

It is rare, and so is Haley Lynn Gray's depth of expertise, practice, results and hours invested over many years in understanding this enigma called Marketing.

This book provides a comprehensive set of guidelines to erect your own big top for your business. The more poles, the more sturdy the structure.

The steps are logical and numbered. You can begin by scanning the whole book by chapter and subtitle to get a clear overview of what you need to know to erect your own tent.

Now you are ready, so begin, hungry to understand, absorb and apply the concepts in this book. You richly deserve the success you desire.

Leslie Thomas Flowers

International Best Selling Author (Amazon2018)
Own Your Purpose and Realize Your Potential
Experts Recount their Adventures to Success
Best Selling Author (Amazon 2014)
Champion. 21st Century Women.
Guardians of Wealth & Legacy

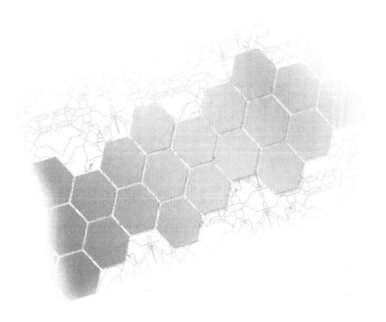

Your 8-Figure Business Blueprint

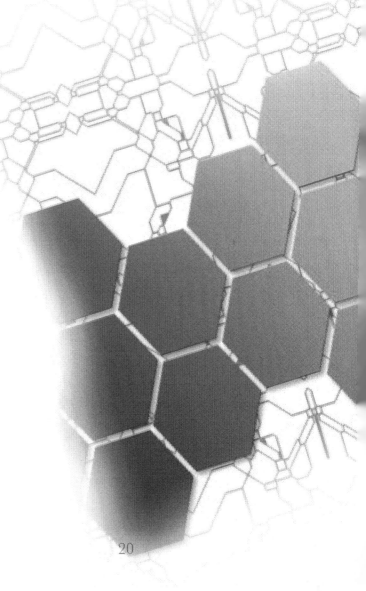

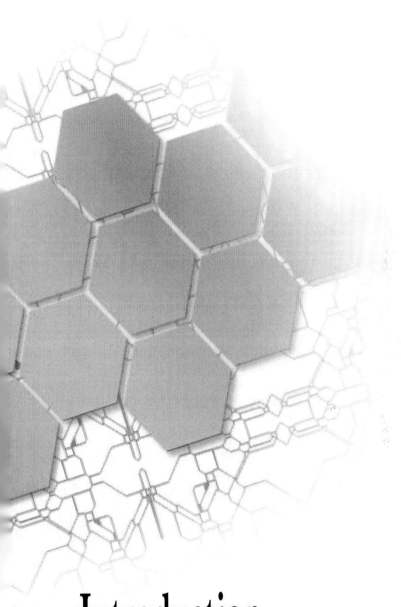

Introduction

"Foundations are key to your growth at any level."

Introduction

Where are your yearly business sales today?
A. $0 to $300,000?
B. $300,000 to $1,000,000?
-or-
C. $1,000,000 to $10,000,000?

Whichever category you're in, this book can help you maximize growth to realize 8-figure sales, and beyond, which puts you in a first class seat to success.

At each point in your business, whether you're netting $4,000 or $4,000,000, your needs change. Sometimes a bit, sometimes a lot, but the foundation pieces remain the same for all levels.

If you don't get the foundation pieces right, then it will be harder to scale your business as you grow. You need to pay attention to what you need to be doing at each step along the way. Make sure that you have your foundations in place, and running well, before you proceed to more complicated maneuvers.

Foundations are key to your growth at any level.

As you get all the foundation pieces working in your favor, you'll notice how much easier some things become. In monitoring specific areas of your business, and realizing full potential in those areas, you'll achieve greater results with less work. You won't spend time spinning your wheels, you'll be laser-focused on the key areas that count, the ones that result in sales. No more spending hours on tasks which give you little results. You'll understand exactly what to do, how to do it, and how to grow your business to new heights.

I want to point out that you don't need to do everything at once, nor do you want to try! That would be insanity, and you'll drive yourself nuts if you do everything on a given day. Get the foundation pieces going first, before you attempt the more complex tasks. I'll walk you through that in the following sections. Follow the plan, and the plan will work for you.

This book is aimed at small business owners, attorneys, chiropractors, dentists, optometrists, and other professionals who want to step up to the next level but seem stuck by the confines of their daily routines. I'll show you how to manage your situations to get the most out of every sales-generating idea.

~ Haley Lynn Gray

"Those people you endear
will be your champions
and cheerleaders."

A word about getting started.

When you first start your business, you're going to notice that you need to spend most of your time marketing, selling and talking to people. Give yourself a goal for the number of people you will touch per week, and focus on talking, touching base, and interacting with as many people as possible.

This is not necessarily to sell them on your products or services, because if you act too desperate, people can tell, and they will run, as far, and as fast away from you in the opposite direction as their legs will carry them. You know those people who try to sell everyone they meet. They are piranhas and you don't want to be a piranha.

Instead, focus on building referral networks, and connections, and the business will come. Build the know, like, and trust factor, and people will buy from you and refer you to others. By not coming across as desperate, and as someone who is real, you can forge the bonds that will make a real impact on your business. Those people you endear will be your champions and cheerleaders. They'll remain lifelong friends and associates, so that in 10 years from now, you'll be grabbing a coffee or beer with them, and you'll say, "Hey, remember when we met? Seems like a lifetime ago. We've had some crazy times along the way."

Those are the people you want promoting your business.

Your Checklist:
- Determine: Ideal Client, Target Market and Service (what you do; what you sell; who you sell)
- Define Your Brand, Business Name and Logo
- Define Your Core Business Values
- Build Your Website.
- Build Your Online Presence.
- Place Ads on Google, Yahoo, Bing, et. al.
- Join Networking Groups
- Set Budgets for Marketing and Advertising
- Set up CRM and Sales Process
- Determine End-to-End Analysis
- Market, Market, Market!

First things first.

As my friend and mentor Annelies Gentile has said, "First things first." That is particularly pertinent in business. I have been the poster child of rushing in without doing much (okay, any!) research and just hoping that something will to stick. Don't do it. It's a trap.

What that got me was lost revenue, frustration, and a whole lot of pain.

It can work for some industries, like say, house cleaning, particularly because they don't require a lot of education, have low regulatory hurdles, and you don't have to deal with tons and tons of government regulation. They are also niche and word-of-mouth. In some industries, you can find yourself making a fair amount of money before you must start really thinking about marketing, scaling, or what you're doing.

Many other types of businesses are subject to a fair amount of government regulation, and rules. So, you may be subject to things like laws requiring licenses, certification, and insurance which all drive up the cost of doing business significantly. Those businesses need more intensive research and tools to measure and plan for success.

By taking a step back in your business, at the beginning, and doing periodic assessments along the way, you can decide if you're on the right track, and if the business is working the way you want it to.

First, you need to know your numbers like the back of your hand. You need to understand what 10 minutes means in dollars for your workday, and what an increase in rent or insurance does to your bottom line. You need to understand how your business functions, not just let your accountant, Quickbooks pro, or low-skilled office manager handle it for you. You must understand it.

Once you know your numbers (and you must continually reassess them), then it's time to look at your vehicles for gaining sales. What are your marketing and sales efforts to grow your business? There's not a business out there that doesn't relish more sales.

Are you making the sales you want? If not, then it's time for a course correction. It's okay, almost every single business out there evolves and changes over time. Pepsi, Coke, Apple, IBM, and even your local diner all change a bit here and there, depending on market conditions, and where they think they'd like to go with their business.

I think a lot of times we have it stuck in our heads exactly what our business is, and what our story is going to be, but businesses, are frequently living, changing, growing things.

I believe that a business is either growing and changing, or it's withering and dying.

Which one is your business?

In this book, we're going to talk about what you need to do from a marketing perspective to go from 0 to 8 figures (if you'd like to grow it that big). We're going to discuss the concepts, but also the processes you need to have in place to grow your business to where you need it to be, then to where you'd like it to be.

"Start with the end in mind," ~Stephen R. Covey

If you can begin with the end in mind, the pieces will make a lot more sense. What is your end? Think of it now. What is the number, right now, that is your result? Don't be afraid to make changes to make that outcome happen.

You need to decide what you want your business to be, before you ever begin. Do you want lots of income? Multiple revenue streams? How much do you want to work? How many people do you want working for you? What are YOUR needs from this business?

I have heard it said several times that for the first $250K/year your business makes, you market constantly. After that point, you focus on systems and processes. I have found that to largely be true.

That's why I focus on both the marketing, but also the systems and processes that support the marketing, so that you're not losing money along the way, or wasting money on ads that don't bring you the outcome you seek.

Build the systems as you go and keep improving them so that you can GROW your business.

In the next **18 Facets of Fearless Marketing,** I'll walk you through everything you need to know to set up those systems and improve their performance. These will help realize actual growth and attain the sales results you desire. Through these 18 Facets of Fearless Marketing, you can achieve any goal you desire, if you just put into practice the tools offered here.

I would wish you "good luck," but business success isn't luck, it's knowing what to do, how to do it, and working smarter, not necessarily harder.

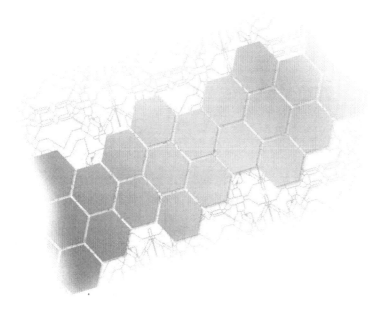

FEARLESS MARKETING
Your 8-Figure Business Blueprint

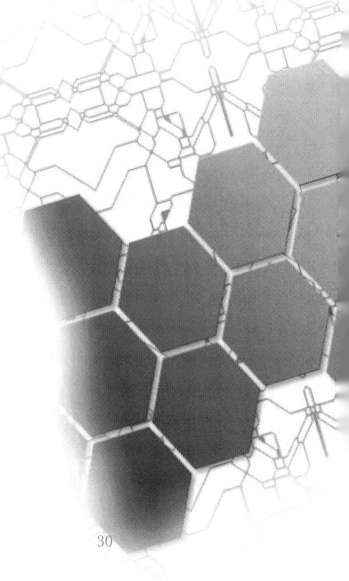

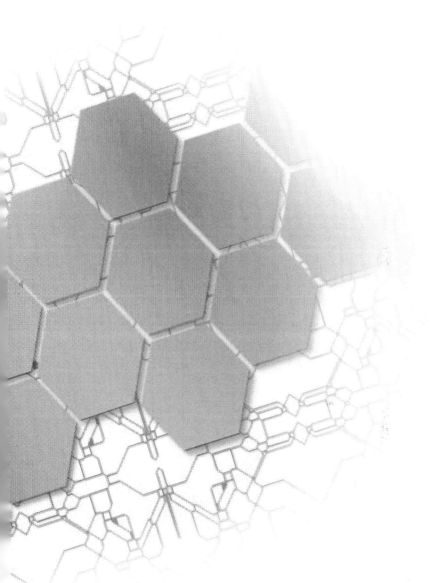

1. WHO DO YOU SERVE?

"*Words are critically important in your marketing efforts. Use them wisely.*"

1. Who do you serve?

Who is it that your business serves? Too often, I hear from small business owners, that they can help anyone. Many lawyers will take any case that comes their way, whether it's a traffic ticket, a will, a divorce, and the list goes on. They spread themselves thin, and dabble in various aspects of law, just to get paid.

This will work to some extent. You'll get clients, and some will be great, but some will be not so great. It's vital to pay attention to service offerings and the clientele that desires those offerings. Think about it for a minute. Do you want to take lots of lower margin clients, or do you want to take fewer, more exclusive clients, who can afford to pay your rates?

I remember sitting in a networking meeting when it hit me like a lightning bolt: you need to be specific! And, the more specific, the better.

A networking partner in that meeting works for one of those companies that sends out packets of coupons in the mail. He described how his best referral is take-out restaurants and pizza joints. He explained, it's the moms who open these coupon packets, usually over the recycling bin. They decide in a split instant whether to keep a coupon or toss it, based on whether it's something that they will use or not.

He pointed out that pizza and take-out restaurants do well, because these are typically moms of kids—frequently pre-teens or teenagers—who have a ton of activities going on in their lives. This correlates to the family ordering take out or delivery at least once or twice per week. Mom is busy shuttling kids around and she doesn't have the time to make home cooked meals. She wants those coupons!

He tells this same story week after week, and people know to refer pizza parlors and take-out joints to him. He's made his referral relatable and specific. We see the mom and we know she needs help with dinner.

It also hits home for me because I'm that mom. I have 4 active kids, with too many activities to count- Scouts, Tae Kwon Do, sports, choir, and the list goes on. We end up eating out at least a couple of times per week. Take out is a thing in my house, because we're constantly on the go, going at least 4 different directions at once.

We all understood why he told the story, because it invoked a clear picture of his ideal client. Those are exactly the types of people that the restaurants want to target: busy families who eat out regularly and become regular customers.

Suddenly it all started to make sense in my head. We need a clear picture of our ideal client. We need to see him or her in our heads and be able to describe them to others.

I applied this principle to my business by getting super specific about the kinds of clients I do and do not look for. I began telling stories in my marketing geared toward those ideal clients, and suddenly things took an amazingly positive turn. Clients started flowing in my door. The exact type of clients I wanted. It was eerie.

What I learned is that people must be able to see themselves as your customer before they ever have the first conversation with you. They must be able to envision themselves as someone who uses your products or services. They must envision themselves as your client. If they can't put themselves in those shoes, then they won't bother to take the conversation to the next step.

Before I got super specific about what I wanted in my clients, I touted myself as an expert for female entrepreneurs. I knew I could help women achieve more, but that was also a pitfall. Every female is not necessarily a good client for me.

This theory about hyper defining clients explains to me why working with just "female entrepreneurs" was never going to be enough in my marketing. It's like saying that I work with anyone with ovaries. Just because you have a segment defined, make sure that it's defined ENOUGH. Female entrepreneurs is a broad market. They could be in direct sales, attorneys, chiropractors, or they could be selling products on Etsy. They could be owners of small businesses, with just themselves, or they could be the head of a large corporation. Needless-to-say, the message of working with just women wasn't connecting to anyone. By trying to connect to MORE people, I was connecting with fewer people.

With whom do I work? I work primarily with attorneys and other licenses professionals who want more clients coming through the doors for their businesses.

What if I scare someone off? Well, it turns out that the opposite happens.

When I got specific about my asks, and described my current projects, suddenly lots of small business owners could see themselves working with me and took the leap to schedule a call. Attorneys found out that I understood their needs and industry. I got referrals from other lawyers, and people who knew lawyers turned them on to me. I became known as the go-to for that market segment.

And so, it began.

Narrowing down your niche is critical to growing your business. You can go to the extent of building an ideal client avatar, but you don't necessarily need it quite that precise. By understanding the problems, needs, wants and desires of your ideal client, and making it the focus of your marketing, you can craft a message that will resonate with the right audience. You will pull them in, so that you can start the conversation with them.

So, who do YOU serve? Take some time and think about who it is exactly that you serve. I'm pretty sure it's not really everyone between the age of 20 and 90 with skin, and if it is, then maybe you need to narrow it down a bit.

What is this thing called a client avatar?

There is a branch of branding that revolves around creating your ideal client avatar. It is basically a fully built out profile of your ideal client or customer. Are they male or female? How old are they? What are their hobbies, education levels, income, and how many children do they have, etc.?

A client avatar is typically told as a story about a person who is using your product and is a somewhat but perhaps not entirely fictitious creation that determines how you do your marketing. It's a representation of the ideal client and should be as specific as possible. Clothes, hair, habits, lifestyle, home, cars, education, vocation, vacations, etc. Try to imagine as much as possible.

I find that the more detailed you get is useful because you start to understand where the person hangs out, what kinds of things they like (and don't like), along with lots of ideas of things they may react to. Where it's generally helpful is with edge cases.

For instance, most people who like golf have heard of Jack Nicklaus or Tiger Woods. But many people (like me) who aren't particularly into the sport also tend to know them. So, if you're using Tiger Woods or Jack Nicklaus to find avid golfers, that might not be the best tool. However, I bet if you talked about Patrick Reed (the 2018 Masters' winner), then you are more likely to find people who are avid golfers.

What kind of market research should I be doing?

In general, the more that you understand about your target market, along with the words that they use to describe their problem, the more successful your marketing efforts are.

Learn to speak their language.

Along with creating an ideal client avatar, I also would get a group of current or former clients together to listen to the words that they use to describe their problems. No current clients? Then get a group of people together in a networking group, or people who you think might be a good match for your ideal client.

I know it's not easy to accomplish, with logistics and all, but take the time at the beginning of your business, to interview 5-10 clients or client-substitutes so that you can start to know what language they use. You'll reap untold benefits.

Think of it this way: ask someone what their main problem is. And, if they say, "My 20th high school reunion is coming up, and I'd like to look great in my photos, to tone up, and look awesome," then, the answer isn't, "Oh, so you want to lose weight?"

No, it's definitely not. Because that isn't what they said. They said that they wanted to look "great" and "awesome," and "tone up" for their 20th high school reunion.

By taking time to write down the actual words that people use to describe both their problems, AND the desired outcomes, you can match the words in your marketing efforts and more effectively reach your desired audience.

"Words are, of course, the most powerful drug used by mankind."
~RUDYARD KIPLING

Likewise, ask them what they really want. I'm going to go out on a limb here and guess that if you ask a small business owner what they want, they will answer that they want to go on a cruise to Alaska, or go to the Caribbean, pay for my kid's college, or maybe they'd like to buy a new Lexus. Chances are, most people are NOT going to say, "I want $30,000."

People want money, but that isn't the result they're seeking. Likewise, if you're a divorce attorney, people don't really want the divorce. They want to be free, and they want the pain to stop. They want the problem to go away. The divorce is the tool they use to get their desired result.

Words are critically important in your marketing efforts. Use them wisely.

What are my core business values?

Your core business values are going to fundamentally shape your business, and your life. Are you a luxury brand? Are you religious? Do you close every Sunday?

It has become much more common for businesses to make part of their mission to give back to the community. One example is TOMS shoes. For every pair of TOMS that's purchased, a pair is donated in Africa. That mission and value statement is built into the very core of the business.

It has become progressively more common for for-profit companies to give back a significant percentage of their income to charity, or to a cause, or a mission. Not that all companies do this, or should do it, but there are some that do.

Core business values can also be expressed in many ways. Are you a small, local business, without employees, or do you want to grow your business and franchise it? Are you about sustainability? How about giving to local charities, children's hospitals, or the arts? How much do you value money or prestige? What is important to you?

It's important to understand how you interact with your customer base and to determine if they seek you out because of your core values. Would they choose you over your competition based on your core values?

These are important questions to begin to consider and answer as you're formulating your business position.

A couple of years ago, I decided that I was going to grow my business slowly, with a tremendous focus on providing exceptional customer support for every client. I aim to provide high quality marketing strategy and support with outstanding service.

I differentiate myself from many other marketing businesses, because I give my clients honest answers to the questions of what is working and what isn't, and what is likely to work and what isn't. In fact, if an ad campaign isn't working, I will let them know quickly, before we spend hundreds or even thousands of dollars on something that is not likely to even produce results. I will give people truthful feedback, even if it means that they'll never buy from me or I make less money.

This philosophy has been a conscious decision on my part. But, I'll clue you in, it's not always an easy one! However, it's how I've set myself apart and formulated my business plan.

Why do you care about core values?

It used to be that people would just start a business, and set up shop, and nobody worried about core values, who you are, or what you stand for. But, core values are key in today's climate.

It doesn't matter if you're a multi-billion dollar per year company, like Chick-fil-a, or if you're a small business just starting up, like Wine & Design. Your core values are going to impact everything you do.

Unfortunately, as Walmart, and other companies have discovered, being a huge conglomerate, and trying to come across later as socially responsible by changing their core mission and values, especially after a major incident, comes across as fake. People don't necessarily accept what you say, just because you say it.

Think about it. When you go to Walmart, you expect lots of cheap stuff. You don't necessarily expect the products you buy to be exclusive or quality. You also expect to run into all kinds of unique people (hence, the "people of Walmart" slideshows on social media). The paint is going to be grays and blues, the lights are going to be a harsh fluorescent, and the lines are almost always going to be long.

You just KNOW that the employees aren't particularly happy to be there. They show up to do a job. It pervades almost every aspect of the business. It's not a pleasant shopping experience, but you get cheap stuff and save money.

So, when Walmart started a campaign a few years ago talking about sustainability, and how they select their products based on sustainability, it read as "hype." In fact, it was laughable and not credible in the least. I'm not sure that many people believed any or part of it. It was lame attempt to join the "sustainability crowd."

It's a lot like trying to close the gate after the horse got out. That pony is long gone!

Instead, look at a company like TOMS. They donate one pair of shoes for every pair purchased. They always have. That's how they built their reputation. The desire to give back has been inherent to the business since day one. You know TOMS, and you pay more for TOMS, because a child in Africa is going to get a pair of shoes.

Now, your core mission and values don't have to be that extreme, but you do need to stop and think about what you're doing and why. Not just to make money in business, but determine HOW you're going make money. Your core values should permeate your business.

For instance, will you be closed on a certain day of the week? Is there anything such as a donation or benefit to others tied to your sales? Will you hire people with disabilities or from a certain minority segment, or military background? Do you want to be a solopreneur, or do you want to have hundreds of people working for you?

There are more questions to ask than I have space in this book but use these as jumping off points. Think about all aspects of your business and how they're tied to your core values.

When I started Leadership Girl, I did so with the notion and the idea that we need to support one another in life, in our choices, and in our businesses. There are plenty of very large corporations out there, but the focus on helping small business, and women in leadership is a new one.

Opportunities lack for most women to be mentored by other, powerful women. I want to foster the discussion between all women for building each other up and helping each other succeed. I believe that leadership is a very necessary skill whether you are in a corporate position, or whether you are a leader of a small business. That ethos is woven into every aspect of my business.

How do I set my prices?

One of the biggest challenges in business is price setting. It sets the tone for everything else. This isn't a strictly marketing facet; it's part of your business from end-to-end. Prices affect how you market your business and they determine the overall tone.

Do you want to be a luxury brand? Or more accessible, where you make less profit per transaction, but make up for it in volume?

That is a critical distinction, and will make a huge difference in your branding, and in your messaging. Getting pricing right is CRITICAL in your business, because it determines whether you can hire employees and scale up, or not. It will differentiate between you being able to afford to vacation and living hand-to-mouth.

You also need to calculate your billable hours. That is, how many hours per day, and per week you can bill clients for your services.

For instance, if you are a website designer, even if you have a full load of work, you may only be able to bill four hours per day, because the other four hours per day are spent marketing, working on administration, etc.

Or if you are a massage therapist, you may only want to see four or five clients per day because of the physical demands of the practice.

Your prices need to reflect how many hours per day you can realistically bill your clients, and account for what you need to be making to pay your bills. This is where understanding your accounting numbers is key. You MUST know your break-even point, profit margin, and the like.

Let's look at a couple of case studies.

Christian Louboutin is a shoe maker of luxury women's shoes, and the company has a trademarked red sole on the bottom of their shoes. To those who know anything about women's shoes, they are one of the top luxury shoe makers with shoes ranging in price from hundreds to many thousands of dollars. There are some people who collect these shoes and see them as a massive status symbol. They are known for their elegance and craftsmanship.

Let's contrast Christian Louboutin to Nike.

Night and day. While Nike does command a bit of a premium price, I think it's fair to say that currently, their tennis shoes don't go for thousands of dollars. Instead, I buy my kids Nike shoes at places like Rack Room shoes, where I can get the buy 1 pair, get 1 pair 50% off, and for children's shoes, they range in the $50 price range.

Nike shoes typically hold up for a few months for kids, and maybe more for adults, but I don't exactly equate the brand with high quality craftsmanship and long-lasting durability. They are predictable, durable shoes that my children have worn through the mud and gunk many times over. (And trust me, I'd cry if someone treated a pair of Louboutin shoes the same way!)

As you build your business, be aware of how your pricing will affect your brand positioning as well as your bottom line.

What's in a Brand?

Most people have thought that a brand is your logo, and that's about it. The reality is that branding is your logo but more. It's the look, feel and language of your marketing. It's centers around the user experience, and how your company speaks to your clients, vendors and employees. It's your identity.

How it Looks Matters

Too often I see small businesses fall into a trap where their marketing and branding materials aren't consistent. They're not even close. They use different logos in different places, and the colors aren't pulled through to other aspects. The words aren't thematic, and the images or photos vary from place to place. In fact, the whole look is a disjointed mishmash.

I've had clients and friends who identified themselves as "7-Figure Coaches" or, "7-Figure Business Owners." But their image hasn't always been consistent with that tagline. That can be a problem when it comes to credibility. If you are telling people that you are making a ton of money, and advertising that you can take them to the same heights, then your branding, website, and promotional materials need to reflect that same quality. Otherwise, people aren't going to believe you.

Anyone can SAY they're a 7-figure earner, but unless their brand looks like it, people will know it's a just a farce.

If you say you're a 7-figure earner, people want you to look a certain way. If you don't, they're going to judge you poorly and pass you by.

Likewise, with trendy or splashy themes. It is far better to be simple, professional, clean, and corporate, rather than do something that doesn't look quite so professional, because you were trying to stand out. There are, after all, a finite number of things that you can do with a website and materials.

People will come to recognize you by the name of your business, your logo, website, and even the photos you use. If your website looks like it was done by third graders, people are going to wonder about your business credibility. Font, images, photography, layout, writing, etc., all come into play with how your website is perceived. It needs to look professional and organized.

It's better to have a more dated website than one that looks poorly done.

Nowadays with so many free and easy to use tools, there's really no reason why you can't have a professional looking website for minimal or no cost. Seriously, you can just fill out an easy to use template from **WIX** to create a perfectly beautiful and functional site. And, it requires about the same skill level that you would need to edit a word document.

Ok, I get it, you're not the savvy tech kind. That's okay, you can hire out your first website for a few hundred to a couple thousand dollars.

Keep the look between your website, logo, business cards, brochures, advertising and marketing materials consistent. That means, use the same fonts, logos, and colors everywhere. Where possible, you may even decide to use the same pictures in various places.

What factors are key in developing a consistent look to your marketing efforts?

Use a consistent font style and consistent font size (barring headlines or subheads) across everything you do. Use coordinating and similar pictures that convey similar messages. Use the same colors for your text, backgrounds and other artwork.

Eliminate pictures and text that contrast greatly or don't align or fit well in the space. Stop using too many colors, or too few. Don't use your own pictures or a do-it-yourself logo. Errors like these give a bad impression.

Professional or semi-professional photography is key. You don't want images with poor lighting or bad focus. Hire a professional photographer who understands business-setting lighting, or purchase stock images. Always use a professional photographer for headshots for you and your staff.

Hire a professional designer to create your logo. (Yes, you need one.) Don't use one of those do-it-yourself logo builders. You'll look like everyone else.

Check out what your competition is using, to see what works and what doesn't. Chances are, you'll see a ton of similar logos because many have used the identical logo builder programs.

In the case of a website, it needs to have one clear call to action. In most cases that call to action is the prospect contacting the business to learn more. Too often people try to put multiple calls to action on their home page, which usually results in people doing exactly NONE of them.

Your website is more than an extension of your brand, or a place to showcase your products and services, it should press upon your visitors to act.

You want a cohesive brand that flows out effortlessly from your marketing materials and website.

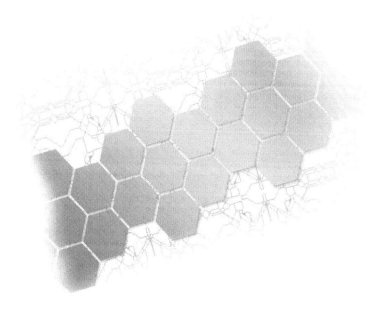

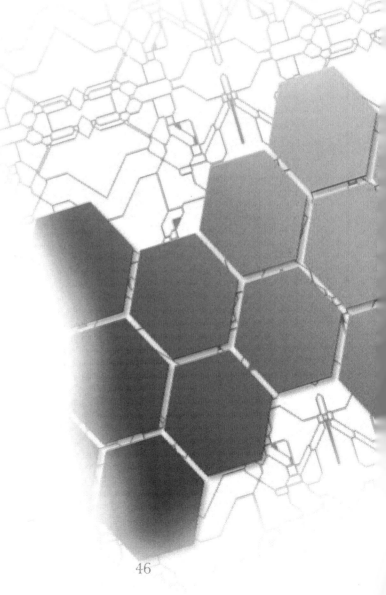

FEARLESS MARKETING
Your 8-Figure Business Blueprint

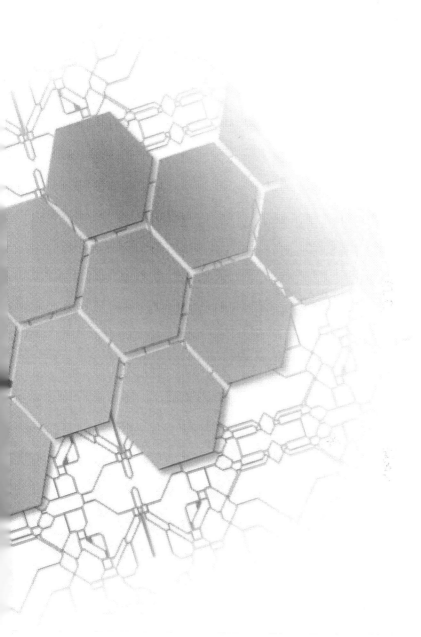

2. End-to-End Analysis

"Most clients are a
one and done
kind of deal."

2. End-to-End Analysis

What does your customer flow look like?

Most people look at their business, and they see the client come in for their appointment, experience the benefits of you as provider, and then leave when finished, going back to their lives. It's a simple transaction: in>work>out.

But, what if you were potentially leaving a LOT of money on the table? What if I told you that looking at the end-to-end picture from having people out there wandering around in their lives, wondering what service they need, to when they become clients of yours and using your expertise, and even after their experience with you, there are tons of opportunities for repeats, upsells, and complementary products and services?

There are. Through the entire process you can find ways to make more money per client by massaging that relationship and selling a broader product and service base to that client. It's always cheaper to sell another service to an existing client than it is to sell a service to a prospect.

Case Study: Home Inspection

For most people, purchasing a home is one of the largest purchases they will make. Most people find a realtor, who refers their clients to a home inspector or home inspection company for the home inspection.

The home inspector inspects the home, and provides a detailed report, and their job is done.

Most clients are a "one and done" kind of deal. They don't tend to repeat, unless they are making purchases on investment properties.

It's a pretty simple process. Clients come in, you service them, and then send them on their way. Opportunities for repeats are few and far in between.

The place where a home inspector is going to have repeat business is through partnerships. While individual homeowners may need an inspection every five years or so, a home inspector can garner repeat business through a partnership with a complementary business, such as a Realtor.

Home inspector and Realtor join forces, and suddenly the real estate agent has a knowledgeable and reliable person to perform their inspections, thereby preventing ugly surprises with the other side's inspection report. As an agent, if I know my guy or gal isn't going to miss anything, then I'm confident that the deal is more likely to go through. By using an inspector who I have a relationship with, I know that I can count on them to give me a trust-worthy report.

As the home inspector, I'm thrilled, because my agent is a great source of jobs for me. I get consistent work. It's a win-win.

That's how one makes repeat business work in an industry that is used by the consumer on an infrequent basis. Find a complementary partnership and forge a solid, working relationship.

Case Study: Attorney

Contrast a home inspector with an attorney. The attorney will also get a referral from the real estate agent. The attorney will help a client with a closing on a property.

He will do the title search, the paperwork for a closing, and then conduct the closing on the property.

Just like the home inspector's referral client, the attorney's business could be done when the transaction is done, because unless he or she is creative, there's not a lot of opportunities for upsells, or repeat business with clients, since a home purchase is something that most people only do a few times in their lifetime, and they tend to use whomever the realtor recommends.

But what if...

What if that same attorney builds an email list with former clients and leads, and offers them other, complementary services? What if they offer wills and estate planning? Many people who are purchasing a home are doing so because of a change in their lives. They are having children, getting married, upsizing, downsizing, etc., all reflecting changes in their lives.

Those are opportunities to remind clients that it's time to update their wills and estate plans. It might be time to put together a trust for minor children and appoint guardians. Perhaps prepare for other life events.

And once someone has become an estate planning client, they can become a client for life.

How?

The attorney sends out yearly reminders to get an "estate check-up." During the check-up, the attorney can recommend alterations to the estate based on any changes in the law that have happened in the last year.

The attorney can also use a Q&A to determine other legal needs while in the office. Did they have another child, did a parent die, did their living situation change, did they purchase a business or a vacation home?

Or—and this important—are they about to do one of these things? People can make rash decisions without legal counsel, and the attorney can remind them that pitfalls can be avoided if they "run things by" him or her *first*.

There are many life changes and future changes for which clients will need their attorney. These check-ups forge relationships and prove value to their clients, as well as ferret out needs for other services.

There are tons of opportunities to keep clients and make sure they return repeatedly for life, if you seek out those offerings carefully.

Analyze every step of your business.

I know you're going to exclaim, "But this is a book about marketing!"

It is true that this is a book about marketing, but marketing doesn't just happen when you are trying to get people to buy from you in the first place. It's not just about filling your sales pipe and getting people in initially. I feel it's vital for your overall marketing plan to encompass all aspects of your business.

What I'm discovering as I analyze businesses, is that there are many opportunities for follow ups that don't happen, or opportunities for upsells, cross sells, and even downsells, but we rarely use them.

What do those term mean?

An **upsell** is selling upgraded or more expensive products or services to an existing or prospective client.

A **cross sell** is selling different products to an existing client.

And, a **downsell** is offering different and usually less expensive products or services to potential customers who have declined your offerings. This is mostly on the internet.

Successful upselling, cross selling and even downselling, to a certain extent, rely on you, the business owner, to know your customers and clients. What do they want? How are they most likely to get it? When do they want to buy each of your products and services?

How will you know the answers to those questions?

As we talked about in the previous chapter, the best way to learn about your clients is to talk to you clients. Ask them questions. Find out what motivates them. Figure out when they are most likely to purchase.

The best time to pitch a new service or product is after a "win." Whatever that looks like in your industry, it's basically that initial success and generated high in your client's mind after you've serviced them well. That's the best time for them to be eager to "get more."

You can think of it like a drug. They just got a great high and they're enjoying the feeling. They're in a terrific mood. Don't push them out the door, pitch them on the next high.

Many of my health and wellness practitioners have thriving practices, but they'd like to have more clients, and more repeat clients. They want to make more money, but there is a rote process to getting clients, treating clients, having them get well, and then, sadly, having them go on their merry way.

Lather. Rinse. Repeat. Around, and around it goes.

But, what if it didn't have to be that way? Seriously, it doesn't have to be that way.

What if those same businesses could generate a ton of cash flow in their businesses by following a few simple, tried and true steps?

> **1.** Collect email addresses and cell phone numbers from all clients.

> **2.** Send out periodic emails and SMS to their clients, offering them a birthday discount, or perhaps a little gift?

> **3.** What if you could just get more of your clients to show up to their appointments? You'd be making a lot more money, right? Adding appointment reminders and finding out the best way to reach each individual client. Some like email reminders, others prefer text or voicemail.

> **4.** What if you sent out newsletters regularly and asked people to share with their friends, and offered a referral bonus?

> **5.** Offering health and wellness classes to clients. You'll add to your perception as a knowledgeable provider.

> **6.** Offering products that are complementary to their treatment, and reminders to reorder on a timely basis.

These are simple marketing steps, that make sure that clients are cared for, yet so often business owners don't think that they have time to follow these steps.

Yet, what if those same exact steps that those business owners followed could double their income, with the exact same customer base?

Do you think *then* they'd be willing to follow them?

It's not just about generating more income, but also providing a better service to your clients. Think about it.

If I've got three problems, and you've solved one, that's great. It's a win. I called you about that one problem, we spent time on it, and I gave you money to solve that one problem. So, the situation is terrific. You've done what you said you were going to do, and I'm satisfied that you solved my one problem, the one I contacted you to fix.

But, even as I'm walking out your door, even as I'm leaving your services, I still have two problems. My two problems and I are taking a hike away from you…and away from your possible solutions.

What if by offering me other services, you could also give me a way to solve my other two problems? You know, the two problems that I didn't tell you about. The two problems that you don't know exist. You could enhance my life by offering me additional services.

How much do you know me as a client? Did you spend time talking with me, not just to pass the time or forge a relationship, but to gather intelligence. And, are you going to use that intelligence to help me?

To think that it's selfish to upsell is to forget that your clients are human. They have needs and wants. Are you meeting those needs and wants? Do you know what those needs and wants are?

But, even before you get them in to find out all those wonderful and amazing things about your clients, did you remind them about their appointment you? You won't be able to discover what you clients need, if they don't show up for their appointments.

If you remind me to come in and get my hair cut, even if I didn't schedule my next appointment, and provide me with a link or a phone number to call, I'm much more likely to do it.

When my hairdresser of many years started using SMS and reminding me to show up for appointments, I started missing a lot fewer appointments.

I'm pretty sure I'm not unique in that aspect. Sometimes my calendar gets the better of me, and once I add in work commitments and other family members, it frankly gets out of control. Go figure, busy mom, with 4 kids going in totally different directions! I appreciate the reminders to show up for my appointments- even a couple of reminders, so I'm on time, or if I have to reschedule, a way to easily reschedule, if that is needed.

People follow the path of least resistance, we know this. What practices do you have in place to make your clients' interactions with you easy?

You must see it from your clients' perspective. They have full days, and full nights. They have work and family obligations, and they want to chill and binge on Netflix or play golf or do a hundred-and-twenty different things rather than "go to an appointment." Even one that they want to attend.

How are you making it easy and wonderful to come in to see you? Not just appointment reminders, but how about benefit reminders? Do they grasp the benefit of coming into your place of business?

As part of your appointment reminder, it would be wise to remind them of what they gain by showing up for their time with you. Use that appointment reminder as an opportunity to succinctly extoll the virtues of your services.

Back to the original point, analyze every aspect of your business.
- Are you making sure to market to your current and former clients regularly?

- Are you sending them newsletters?

- Are you sending them reminders?

- What opportunities are you giving them to purchase from you again and again, and again?

The least expensive client or customer you will ever get is a repeat one!

Analyze your business from end-to-end to figure out where you have missed opportunities for getting more repeat business and go grab it.

Your 8-Figure Business Blueprint

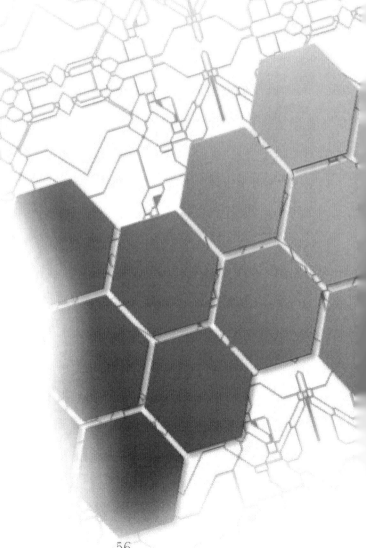

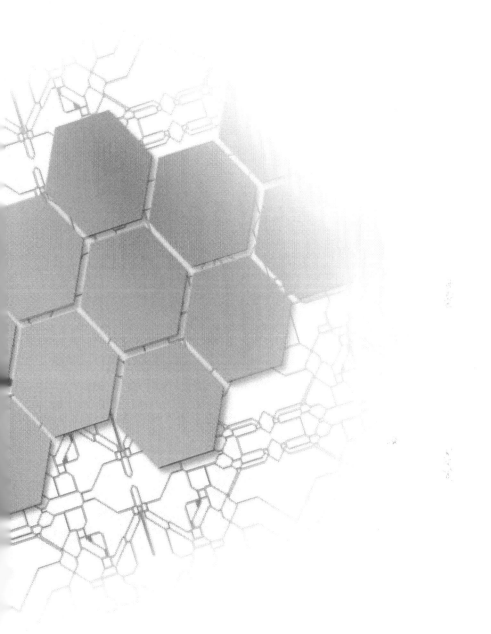

3. Tying All the Pieces Together

"Not everyone is going to have the same learning curve."

3. Tying All the Pieces Together

To grow your business successfully, you're going to need to start putting marketing processes in place early on in your business.

Most of it is easy to do, if you take just some time to figure it out. Or, you can always hire a bit of help. Not everyone is going to have the same learning curve, so you know must know what you can do on your own, and what you need to have someone else complete for you. There is no one way that is right for everyone, because we're each different. Just find the best process for you personally, and work with it.

Email

Set up a series of professional email addresses for your business. Yes. You can keep your Gmail, Yahoo, or even AOL accounts for personal use, but generally, for people to take you seriously, you'll need to create professional business email addresses. This will allow you to have a work address, and a personal address. And, people will respect you for your domain name on your email address.

I suggest that you set up a few different email addresses in your business:

> **1.** Your business professional/public email address, such as your name@yourdomain. This one goes on your business card and will be what you share with everyone in professional settings. Eventually, this email may be managed by someone other than you, so make sure you use this email only for your public connections, not your private ones.

> **2.** Your personal/private email that would be known only to your inner circle. This can be your Gmail, Yahoo, etc, or you can come up with another one using your domain with unbreakable, coded

identifiers such as dragonfire@yourdomain or momsemail@your-domain. You would not want to use president@yourdomain, or other ones that might be guessed by those hunting you down—yes, you'll need to set up your boundaries and privacy from the get-go. Only share this email address with your children's' school, immediate family, close friends, and private connections who need it.

3. Your corporate email addresses such as admin@yourdomain or info@yourdomain for public connection via your website. Eventually, these would be monitored by someone else, or a few different people depending on function and need.

4. Subscription email address. Use subscriptions@yourdomain for any email subscriptions that you might sign up to contact your clients or prospects. Those subscriptions would be for classes, news letters, email blasts, etc.

Remember that as your business grows, things will change. It is best to set up your email as if you were a large corporate entity for your privacy and the efficiency of disseminating information.

A note about salespeople—not yours, the ones trying to reach you to sell you everything from office supplies to a trained workforce. It's important to shield yourself as a CEO would do. Whether you're making $30K, $300K or $3M, salespeople will assume because you own your own business that you are swimming in cash. They figure that all they have to do is get on the phone with you, send you an email, or pop into your office, and you'll be so amazed and excited with their pitch that you'll walk over to that large pile of cash—yeah, right?—and shovel some their way.

So, it's vital that you stick to these four email suggestions religiously. You don't want to end up with every salesperson in the area having direct access to the same email or cell phone number that your kids' school has, or that your significant other has. Keep your private contact information discrete.

This is especially important for your cell phone. If you don't have a landline for your business, get a secondary phone number or cell phone. Keep one for your private connections, and one for your business. Don't put your private number in your email signatures or business cards, either.

You want to make sure you are managing your email volume from day one. I made a huge mistake in signing up for every free offer under the sun when I first started my business. I got lots of free stuff, and a ton of emails in my inbox. In fact, at one point, I think I was getting several hundred emails a day. It was totally overwhelming, and not sustainable at all. Once I figured out the problem, it was almost too late, and I was losing business, because I didn't see the emails I needed to see.

It's easy to miss important emails when you're swamped with other stuff. Keep one email, a Gmail or yahoo or something free and easy, for sign ups, or do like I did: I started unsubscribing from everything from my main emails, and now anywhere that I need to enter my email address, I put in subscriptions@mydomain, so that I still get the emails, and I can go back and search them, but they aren't flooding my inbox anymore.

Once you have your email addresses set up, you'll need to start putting systems in place to manage all the emails you receive. There are tons of different systems out there for managing emails. Some are automatic, others take some steps. See which works best for you.

I find it's helpful to put emails from various senders into separate folders. I set up individual files for each client or business entity. That way, I can go back and see all the emails that each client has sent, as well as anything that I need to address.

I also have folders specifically for things that need to happen today, one for this week, and another for this month, courtesy of an amazing admin with far better organizing skills than I possess. She puts those emails into the folders for me, so I can simply go to that folder to see what I need to address on a given day.

She also takes care of the other hundreds of inbox emails I receive daily. Which, these days, are business-related and professional, rather than the former days in my subscription nightmare. That way, she's determining what needs to be seen by me personally, and what she can handle without my input, thereby freeing up my time for more complex business functions.

If you search the Internet, there are plenty of ways to help manage the volumes of emails you're going to get, and you can put systems in place to address those emails. When marketing using your emails, you're going to want to make sure that you have a good way to manage the influx. Because, once you start marketing this way, you'll get inundated.

Mountains of Business Cards

If you do any amount of face-to-face marketing, you are going to have mountains—and, I do mean mountains!—of business cards. Take the time to file the information you need, by either getting an app to scan the cards, or hiring someone to manually enter the information into your address book quickly.

There is no elegant way to handle the volumes of cards you're going to get, other than to get on top of them, and stay on top of them. You may decide to put them into a file box, or scan them, or manually enter them. There's no right way, only the way that works for you, but keep in mind how you want to access and use those contacts.

The information on the business cards is important. These are people who have shook your hand, have seen your face, and you've spoken to you with at least a few words. Don't treat them as you would grabbing cards off a corkboard in a coffee shop—not that anyone does that. These are part of your warm market. Keep their name, phone number, email, business name and title, and sometimes physical address (although rarer these days). Some people find it helpful to have a point of reference for how you met, or what you talked about. It depends on your business and purpose for networking.

You are going to collect a lot of business cards. Stacks of them. Piles of them. So, organize them.

Enough said.

CRMs, Client Management, & Billing Software

If you have a business where you are bringing in clients, you need tracking software. Yes, you can find some stuff for free, but this is one of those cases where you get what you pay for.

Take the time to understand your business, before leaping in, but don't wait too long.

There are hundreds of different software packages out there, ranging in price from relatively modest to eye-watering. Don't just spend money because someone told you it was the best option. Do some serious research to make sure that it will work for your business, in a way that works for you.

Also, be very, very wary of long term contracts. Some companies are going to want to have you sign a contract for three to five years, and frankly at the beginning of a new business that is just too long. There are plenty of other reputable choices out there for quite less of a commitment.

> *"Don't just spend money because someone told you it was the best option."*

A CRM is a Client Relationship Manager, this helps your sales force track prospects, and know where they are in the lead cycle. You can use a system like Ontraport, Infusionsoft, or Sales Force to act as your CRM.

Initially, you will be using your CRM, but eventually you'll hire someone else to manage sales. I'll go into hiring a sales staff in detail in a bit, but for now let me just say that CRM's are vital for any salesforce. CRM's can track performance and results and give you a vision into your sales team's daily/weekly/monthly/yearly activity. Never, ever hire a salesperson without clearly defined and accepted upon goals and results.

Depending on your business, you may want more functionality, so thinking about where you want to go from where you are now is super important.

1. Do you want to have a sales funnel, where people come to a landing page and get more information about your business?

2. Do you plan to sell other products and services? By building these out, or at least having the capability early on, you will have options to sell to more clients.

3. Do you want to be able to track leads, and get a clear picture as to where you are in the sales process with clients and prospects?

Some pieces of software like Ontraport can also bill clients, but you may have other needs. For instance, if you're an attorney, you need to accept credit card payments only through certain vendors, and certain things like Law Pay are not necessarily already integrated into Ontraport.

It's super helpful to sit down with a pen and paper and draw out what it looks like to get a client at this point in your business. Then, spell out your follow-up processes. And, finally look at what it will be like to get a client a year or two from now. What will change and what will stay the same?

You may not necessarily be able to start on the software that you'll end up using a few years from now, but it could be possible to lengthen the lifespan of your system if you do some solid research. The more you put into the discovery process, and determine which programs address your needs, the longer the program will last and the more efficiently it will perform.

Why in the world are we talking about software when talking about marketing? Because, you're going to need processes in your business. There will come a time early on when you realize that you can't keep track of all your follow-ups. While you could use a spreadsheet, using software is much easier.

It's even easier if you have pre-written email, and SMS campaigns already done, so that you don't have to think about every single email you have to send out. You can either set them, and forget them, or you can edit them as you go, but you have something to start with.

The other piece is client onboarding and moving the client through the process. Do you want to have to remember to send out every contract, and every set of directions? Or you just want to hit a button (or have an admin hit a button) which is "send all the new client stuff?"

And, that's an important point: don't bog yourself down with rote tasks. That's why we have computers. If you have 20 new clients a month, and it takes you 2.5 minutes to copy and paste a pre-written email, address it, attached directions and/or contract to it, that's 50 minutes of your time each month. If you hit a button, and it happens automatically, that's 40 seconds a month.

How much is YOUR time worth?

Make sure you have a way that you can track all your contacts, prospects, and follow-ups. Using a spreadsheet will work for a few months, but I can guarantee that it will be hard to keep current once you have more than about 100 contacts on it. Sorting and managing those numbers will get progressively more difficult.

The amount of time you'll save by having decent software will more than make up for any cost that you incur, provided you don't just jump to software that is thousands of dollars per month. Please don't do that. Get a decent system that's budget friendly.

Bulk Email

Many CRM systems have bulk email capacity built in, but if you don't have a system that allows for bulk emailing, you need to get one early on in your business. This is a **MUST HAVE**.

If you have a very simple business, such as a lingerie store, you may only need something like MailChimp. But if you have a business that is a bit more complex, where you may be doing things like mortgages, real estate, and more, a slightly more elaborate system that allows for customer tracking, along with emails, and landing pages is going to be crucial.

Note: As of the time of writing this book, Mailchimp does have landing page capability, but it does not have a way to add any tracking code such as Facebook Pixels to the landing pages. This is important because if you run ads to send people to your landing pages, and cannot track them, then you are wasting money on ads. Thus, if you will be doing ads, you do not want to use Mailchimp® landing pages, at this time.

My favorite platform is Ontraport, because it allows me all the above functionality plus I can create custom proposals, invoices, send out contracts, create membership sites, and do so much more with a single piece of software. Which saves me time and, of course, money.

The Dark Side of Sales and CRMs

At some point in your business as you grow, you'll likely want to hire sales people. Depending on your business, that will happen at different points, but if you're serious about an 8-figure business, marketing and sales must be part of your life.

When you hire someone, you're going to want to have accountability and metrics associated with what they're doing.

A CRM system can give you insight into what people are and aren't doing. A CRM system allows your salespeople to track leads, contacts, and their daily functions and tasks.

It can be a royal pain to get employees to enter their data. On the one side, sales people don't necessarily want to share all their information in case their territory gets split, and their contacts are given away. On the other hand, not entering the data can be used to obscure the fact that someone isn't doing much with their job.

Given that it can take salespeople months to reliably generate leads and clients, it's possible to see how someone who isn't doing much is going to resist entering their data also, because they don't want to expose just how little they are doing.

Of course, there are also employees who will enter data for activities they haven't completed, and just enter large volumes of information to mask the fact that they aren't making sales calls or connections as well.

I've had employees on all sides of the equation, and I will say that the only way to enforce efficient data entry is to make it a condition of employment. You also must get data metrics for each person who is selling on your behalf so that you can have a good idea of whether they are producing or not.

Remember that you will get exactly what you measure, so if you measure number of calls, you will get calls. People are funny that way. Even if you intended one thing, you may get totally bizarre behavior, because you're not measuring the right things.

Here's a simple example that gives you the picture: if you decide to measure the number of hours spent cold calling in person, it would be tracked by the salesperson's time away from the office. Unfortunately, you might get an employee who is sitting at Starbucks scrolling through Facebook, not doing a blasted thing for your sales. But, they're registering as performing well via the matrix of hours away from the desk.

"When you hire someone, you're going to want to have accounability."

I recommend measuring the number of contacts, so that you can have some sort of idea if they are making enough touches. I also recommend having a view into their calendar, along with measuring actual sales obtained from their efforts. Monitor them as much as possible, but don't bog them down with too much paperwork. A true salesperson make contacts and turns them into sales. They must account for their work, so make them enter their contacts and activity into a CRM, but have an admin fill out any lengthy paperwork.

Remember that it is possible to be doing all the right things, and have the sales cycle take a little while to generate clients. If someone is making contacts, and doing the right things, with marketing, then you should see results eventually, given time.

Billing

Having good billing software is going to be critical in your business. By making sure that you can properly track what you are billing, what your financials are, and aren't, you will also know where you need to invest in your business.

Billing time is also a time to reach out to clients to make sure that their needs are being met, and that they are satisfied. You can incorporate information into the billing process about metrics, results, and opportunities to upsell.

Have you ever noticed how many cable companies will include offers along with their bills? That's because they know that they have your attention when you open the envelope, and you are likely to at least LOOK at the latest offers, if only for a split second. It doesn't take a very high conversion rate before this tactic generates a lot more revenue for your business.

It also means that you're also possibly educating your clients along the way. An educated client is frequently a happy client, and every time you touch your clients is an opportunity to educate and give more information.

So, think about how you are billing your clients. Are you offering them the opportunity to click a link and pay online? Do you automatically draft their accounts?

In today's age of easily customizable templates, it is super easy to customize a message for your clients, along with logos, and other information with the bill. You can include a new product offering, or service. You can include an advertisement, offer a discount, or a special package. The beauty of it is that you don't even need to send out paper invoices, and in most cases, you can have them perform a simple click-on-a-link to pay via credit card, bank draft or PayPal.

Every time you touch your clients, whether it's an invoice, a receipt, a phone call, or any other contact is an opportunity to love on your clients.

Tying Up the Operations Pieces

By connecting all the dots on your customer experience, you will increase your sales. Using proper automation, along with getting creative about how and when you contact your customers, you will see decreased costs and increased sales.

Of course, having things like a CRM, sales processes, invoicing, and all that *STUFF* can seem really overwhelming when you're first starting your business, but they are necessary tools to take your business to the next level. The sooner that you put processes in place, the less time you're going to end up devoting to some of these basic things and playing catchup.

The point here is to be lightweight, but effective.

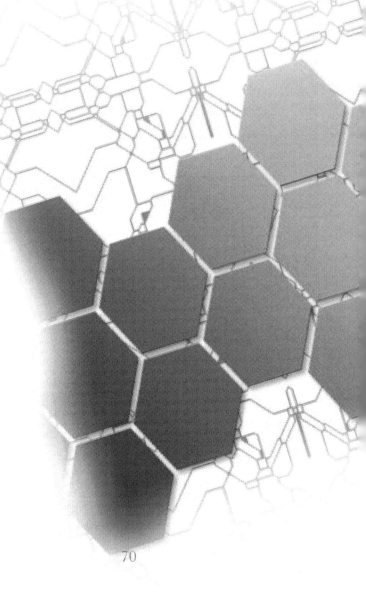

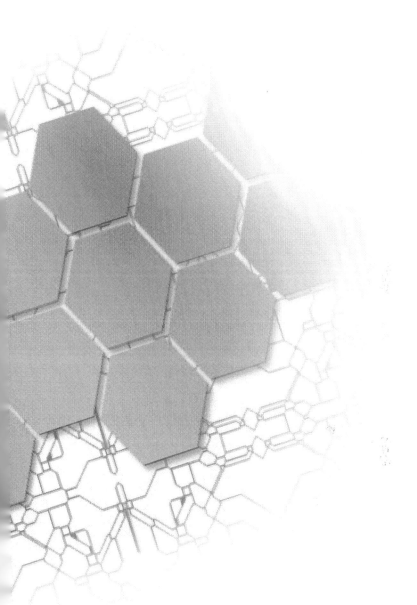

4. Where are you losing clients?

"In life, we only
have 24 hours,
and some of those
must be spent
sleeping."

4. Where are you losing clients?

Let's get real here, all of us drop balls at some points in our marketing processes and end up losing clients by doing so.

From calls that aren't returned, to follow ups that didn't happen, to missed opportunities, this is life. We try our best to avoid losing any viable lead, but we do sometimes drop the ball on gaining possible clients.

Take some time to look at your entire business operation, and identify any place where:

A. You're not following up with leads promptly.

B. You don't have a set timeline and a set process for following up, or you aren't following it.

C. You could be offering clients an additional service, but don't.

D. Follow-up appointments aren't being set, or the next appointment isn't being set at the current one.

E. You're putting on events, but you aren't publicizing them.

F. You aren't asking current clients for referrals.

These are holes in your business and need to be dealt with.

I get it. You're busy. We're all too busy for words.

In life, we only have 24 hours, and some of those must be spent sleeping. If you don't take care of yourself, there won't be a business. Many of us have families. I have four young children, and a house full of pets. Life is hectic, and I always have more that I want to get done in my business and in my life than I have hours in a day. That's just a given.

Decide which things are the most important to you and decide if the loss of clients for things is okay. Prioritize your life in such a way that you account for the balls that are going to be dropped and let that not cause you stress. Being at a child's recital or attending your significant other's art show may be more important than a new client, but only you can make that call. Plan for it, and then be okay with it.

> "*The buck stops with you. You are the one who is going to live with your schedule and with the results of that schedule.*"

And, plan for the stuff that can go. If mowing the lawn on Saturday is keeping you from attending a networking event that could yield potential clients, then it would make more sense for you pay someone else to mow the lawn and avail yourself of business-growing opportunities.

Downtime is important for anyone, but it must be minimized for someone ramping up a business. Watch one or two Netflix shows, but don't binge-watch a season. Play tennis or golf once or a few times a week, not every day. Take a weekend at the beach but forgo the 2-week cruise. Make smart choices with your time.

The buck stops with you. You are the one who is going to live with your schedule and with the results of that schedule. Make sure that your calendar and activities match your desired outcome.

Now, let's look at the ways we lose clients and how we can prevent the fallout.

A. You are not following up with leads promptly.

Determine if this is because you are not responding to emails, or not answering phone calls. You can consider hiring a company to answer the phone, and answer basic questions about your business, before forwarding the information to you. They may even set up a time on your calendar for you to speak. Sometimes a first stage filtering of the calls is enough to reduce call volume.

For emails not responded to, again, you may need to consider having someone answer your emails, and filter through them to determine how you need to answer them. I found with my emails that many of the emails have a standard set of responses and can be categorized in a narrow band of information. I can have a few pre-written emails for many initial inquiries. For others, as I stated earlier, my incredible admin organizes them by priority.

For some types of leads, you may need to automate your response. By using a system such as Ontraport, you can automatically respond, send text messages, and get someone scheduled using automation. It can allow you to give prospects a good amount of attention, without having to spend much of your time on it.

When you think automation, don't think "impersonal." Realize that by automating certain activities, you can provide more personal service to your clients because you are present for them, not rushed because you must set appointments and answer a ton of emails.

Automate the rote processes so you can personalize the service delivery.

B. You don't have a set timeline and a set process for following up, or you aren't following it.

I have a confession to make: I'm good about setting up processes, but not always good about following them through. Okay, I SUCK at following processes.

I'm pretty sure that you aren't going to believe that, unless you know me incredibly well.

That is true, though. But what I've learned is that using a good CRM, which reminds you to follow up, and scheduling time on your calendar to follow up, will help with follow ups. You'll need that system in place, so use a CRM to work on this for you.

Automation can help with follow ups. I have found that if I can schedule follow ups, emails, and almost anything I'm doing, I can get the appearance of more consistency. By putting notes into a good CRM, it can help with using an automated CRM type process, without having it appear to be totally automated.

Follow-through may be hard for you, too, so again, use those automated systems. They are a godsend to me in my business and have helped me go from haphazard to reliable.

C. You could be offering clients an additional service, and don't.

When do you want to offer the additional service?

If it's while you're currently in the middle of doing a massage, it may not feel right to offer more services, or upsell to sell them a longer service, etc. Some people are very comfortable with upsells, but honestly most of us get into our businesses, because we want to help, and we also happen to want to make more money.

What if you could offer an additional service at the time that someone sets an appointment with you?

If you're a massage therapist, you could offer aromatherapy as an additional service at the time that someone books their appointment. By making it either something that they book online, and the additional service is automatically offered that way, or part of your set of questions that you ask when someone books the appointment, you get the opportunity for the sale, without seeming weird about it.

Try finding a natural time to offer additional services, that works for you, and be consistent about it.

If you have staff, and they are not offering additional services, then additional training may be required. Try writing up a script for your staff, so that they can read the script when they handle the phone or conversations with clients.

You may also want to offer a bonus or a prize to staff. A dentist client offered a cash bonus for every whitening treatment her staff sold. It was something they could seamlessly offer while they were cleaning the patient's teeth or performing other tasks chairside, and it was a natural fit with the services. Plus, they offered it to everyone, knowing that a few would take them up on the offer, and when their patients said, "yes," it meant more cash in the pockets of the staff.

Alternatively, you could offer entry into a drawing for a bigger prize, or small dollar amount gift cards. How about winning a prize parking space, or getting your birthday as a paid vacation day?

"Offer additional services, that works for you, and be consistent about it."

You could even get crazy big and make the bonus based on net sales. Having trouble cracking the $2M/year nut? Always hitting the upper $1Ms, but never quite sailing over that $2M mark? Offer to take your entire staff on a cruise if they take the business to the next level. Long-term employees might be able to take their spouses for free, and newbies can buy-in their significant others.

It doesn't have to be a cruise, think outside the box within the confines of your budget and location. An all-inclusive resort, riverboat gambling, a trip to a local tourist spot, Las Vegas, theme park, or whatever it may be, make it an "our" goal and then give them reason to get on board.

Don't be afraid to tie financial gain to upselling for any of your employees. Think of it as an advertising or marketing cost. Just make sure you know your numbers, so you know the amount you can offer them, whether in cash or trips or other things, without hurting your profit margin. As always, check with your CPA to ensure that you or the employee will account for the taxes.

And, remember, your clients benefit from the additional service, or you wouldn't offer it to them.

D. Follow-up appointments aren't being set, or the next appointment isn't being set at the current one.

Setting up the next appointment at the current one, is one of the most important things you can do to fill your sales pipe. This goes for almost every type of business.

The best time to set the next appointment is during the current one. You have a captive audience, they are pleased with your services and products, they like you and your staff…in other words, they're as "bought in" as they're going to get. This is the time to ensure their continued care.

Set the return appointment as you give them their take away. What's the take away? That's the thing they leave with, a token of their visit. It can mean different things to different industries. For some it may mean a detailed treatment plan with free samples. Others it may mean documents to sign and a complimentary pen. Perhaps an article detailing exercises or techniques to improve results. Or, a final spritz of rose water on the face, or smoothing of scented Argan oil in the hair. It's something extra that reminds them you care.

So, before the credit card or checkbook come out, book that next appointment. It's not only for your business, it's for them. You're not being heartless, you're being heartful.

If you are an estate attorney working on wills and estates, scheduling the next appointment in the series will ensure that the process keeps moving forward. You know what the consequences can be if someone doesn't have in place a power of attorney, healthcare power of attorney or will. It can be devastating.

If you are a hairdresser, chiropractor, therapist, esthetician, dentist, or any other type of business that relies on appointments, scheduling the next appointment is critical. It ensures that your clients or patients get the care that they want and need. How can you continue to care for them, to ensure their health and well-being, if they fall off the radar?

I understand. You got into your business to help people and make some money—you don't want to come across as greedy. But look at it this way:

You can't provide the best possible service to your clients, if you don't set their follow-up appointments.

Whatever your appointment-setting method may be, just make sure you have one in place. Your clients will thank you for it.

E. You're putting on events, but you aren't publicizing them.

Events can be a fabulous way to get in front of people. Problem is, if no-one shows up, that doesn't serve anyone well. One of the best ways to build revenue and trust is with classes and events. They are an easy way to get people in the door to get to know you.

One of the health practitioners I've worked with has formed a meetup group, and they do a class once a month with various topics with different specialists coming in. Over time, it has grown. What we saw is that once we started publicizing it a bit more, and pushing on it just a tiny bit, there were more people coming, and better yet, even more clients coming out of the events.

You are an expert in your field and people see that in you. They want to know what you know, but on a smaller scale and geared toward their situation. What three things do your clients, especially new ones, always ask? Okay, you've got your topics, now you can schedule a class.

Think outside the box for these events. Partner with a brewery, a new restaurant or event planners. Cater a lunch-n-learn, an early bird breakfast, or afterwork appetizers. Leverage your networking groups and chamber memberships for venues and audience pools.

Events can be anything: a networking event, a panel discussion, a keynote speaker, or the like.

Events can take place anywhere, just ensure they have ample parking, easy access to major roads, and are handicapped friendly.

Another great benefit of events and classes is that it helps your consumers become more informed. More informed clients means they understand what you're doing and why you're doing it. They "get" your methodology. They have serious buy-in. What do you wish your clients would know? What would you teach them if you had the time? These are subjects for your next round of classes—that you will publicize well.

It's hard to have a split brain, so if you do decide that events, and classes are a thing you want to participate in, make sure you also set aside the appropriate amount of time to publicize them and get the word out. Start with your own clients but open the invite on social media and networking.

F. You aren't asking current clients for referrals.

I get it, it can seem like a drudge to ask for referrals. But if you don't ask, you'll probably not get them. So, take the time to ask your current clients (and hopefully happiest clients) for referrals while they're still happy. Mention specifically what types of referrals are best for your business.

If you are an attorney who does wills, ask for people who have just had a baby for referrals for people who need to get a will in place.

If you are an acupuncturist, ask for friends who have headaches.

If you are a massage therapist, you can ask for people who are experiencing back pain.

Because you mean well, your clients will know you simply want to help others. Tap into what life changes or benefits they've encountered with you. It's that advantage to their life that they can share with others.
Give them a script. No, don't hand them a piece of paper. Frame your ask in a way that allows them to use it as their template for asking friends.

Dentist Example: "Gina, your smile lights up a room. It was my honor to help you look and feel your best. You probably have friends who, like you were previously, don't smile as they should because they are ashamed of what people see. I want to help them, like I helped you. Would you please give me their names and phone numbers or email addresses?"

The more specific you are with your requests, the more likely you are to get those requests filled and met.

Your 8-Figure Business Blueprint

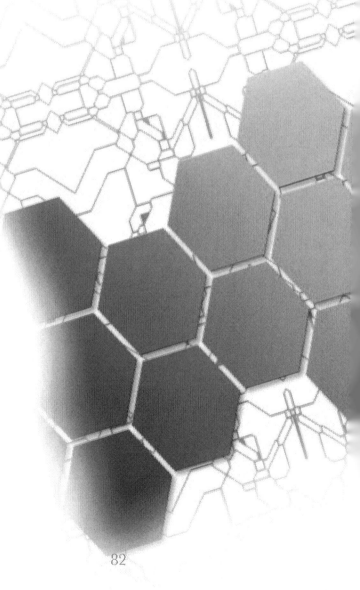

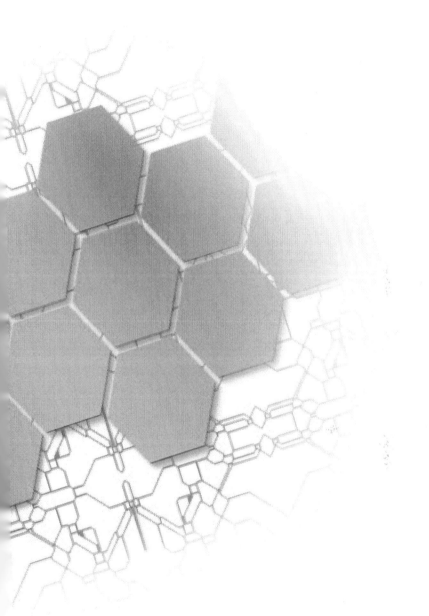

5. Establish your Leadership

"You want to make sure that people know you are "the go-to expert."

5. Establish your Leadership

Establishing your leadership early on in your business is going to be super important. You want to make sure that people know you are "the go-to expert"at what you do.

You might wonder why this is so important, or why I mention leadership at all, as it can be a bit intimidating or off-putting. The idea here is that you want clients to come to you, rather constantly be on the hunt for clients. This is part of my "magic" recipe.

So, how do you do it?

> 1. Share knowledge freely with others, without allowing a free-for-all brain picking.
> 2. Write a book.
> 3. Host a podcast or radio show.
> 4. Serve on a board of directors for a non-profit.
> 5. Facebook Lives.
> 6. Blogging.

There is no end of knowledge. If there were, my brain would have run dry about 3 years ago, and so far, there's no sign of business letting up. In fact, the more I make a point of being genuine, kind, and an abundant fount of useful information, the more people contact me and desire my services.

How do you manage the brain pickers?

With sharing knowledge, come the brain pickers. If you're a doctor, an attorney, a coach, an accountant, or pretty much any type of professional out there, I'm pretty sure you've been approached by a brain picker or three. If you haven't been approached yet, then it's just a matter of time.

I've learned a few strategies for managing this, that usually lead people into purchasing from me, which is a win-win. It builds trust, and it also helps educate them, and brings them to me. What could be better?

If someone asks to pick my brain, I tell them that brain picking sounds painful.

If they just start asking questions, I usually use it as an opportunity to get to know them, and who they are. Since I do business strategy, it's my opportunity to decide if I want to work with them or not. Not all clients are ideal clients, or even great clients.

"With sharing knowledge, come the brain pickers."

A side note about that: sometimes we must be selective with our clientele. Not every person will be a good client. I've fired my share of clients, and my business is better for it. So, be judicious in your search, and don't accept a difficult or ill-fitting client simply because they want to write you a check.

When I'm asked questions from brain pickers, I will answer one or two questions, and give them some hints or tips on what to look for when hiring someone like me. I'll give them questions to ask and do my best to inform them on the services that my business provides. Do I slant things in my favor, paying attention to the things that we do better? Of course, I look at brain picking as an opportunity for me to advertise my services and put myself in the best light.

Brain picking is a chance to get to know people who are possibly considering hiring you. Likewise, if they aren't, it's also an opportunity to weed them out quickly.

Under no circumstances am I rude, but I do get firm with people. If someone wants to go on a deep dive on their problem, I give them information to schedule a session with me and let them know that this is my livelihood. I remind them that this is how I support myself and my family, then I smile, and change the subject.

Is it awkward at times with people who are huge boundary stompers? Well, yes, I'd be lying if I said it wasn't. I've found that with practice that stating something firm and simple, such as, "This is exactly what I do in my business: help people like you get XYZ results. Here's how you can make an appointment." With practice in the mirror and in the real world, it becomes much easier.

If someone gets snippy or rude with you, it's okay to smile and say, "Have a great day," and walk away.

Don't give away the farm. Have a few, well-rehearsed lines ready, and always use it as an opportunity to showcase what you do for your clients. Then, they can set an appointment with you to find out more.

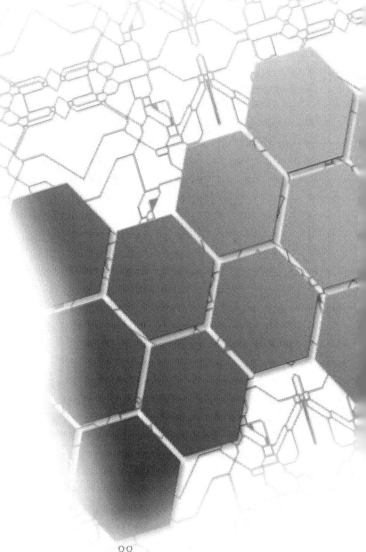

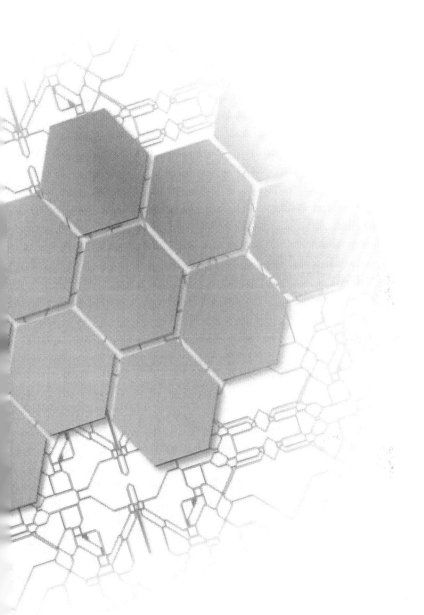

6. Becoming an Author

"I've heard it called the $5 business card."

6. Becoming an Author

Becoming an author sounds incredibly mysterious and scary. But, it's not. You can use a book to show people who you are, what you do, and then use those books as calling cards. The base cost of a printed book is just around five bucks. I've heard it called the "**$5 business card**," and it can be incredibly effective.

If you are not sure what to write, think about problems that your clients, customers, or patients have that you solve. What information do you wish that they had before seeing you? What kinds of data can they bring to you to better help them solve their problems? What are the pitfalls that come with those problems and how can they be managed? Perfect! Now you have the topic for a great book.

It doesn't have to be Tolstoy's *War and Peace*! In fact, the shorter and simpler, the better.

WRITE: You can write the book by typing it into Word (like I have), or you can record it, and have those recordings transcribed. The other option is to use speech to text. Google has a free version that works quite well. Whatever works best for you, just do it.

EDIT: Then, have a good editor edit your book. You can choose whether to have your editor just correct mistakes, or also offer suggestions for better content, or even rewrite portions of your book. You can also have your editor edit it to produce the product you desire. With this book, I chose to have my editor keep it conversational. I didn't want this book to come across as stuffy, proper English, I wanted it to sound real and relatable. More like you and I are having a chat.

FORMAT: After that, have a book formatter design your layout. A well-formatted and designed book is critical to ensure that your message and theme is cohesive. Even though you worked hard on your manuscript and had it edited, professional formatting will help book's audience better understand the content and message of your book.

DESIGN: Next, hire a fabulous graphic designer to create your cover. You want the cover to have the feel of the theme of the book, as well as look enticing and professional. Design is subjective, so don't just hire someone cheaply off the Internet whom you never see. Work with someone you may know from your networking groups or a client of yours. Check out their portfolio first, to ensure that you like their work.

PUBLISH: Most publishing houses will only publish a book from a well-known person. Look at all the politicians, celebrities, news show anchors and talk radio hosts publishing books. They are nationally known figures, and they can command contracts with big houses because they have a large fan base. Self-publishing for a nominal fee is a chance to get your book in print without costing an arm and a leg. There are other options, for larger fees, that come with book promotion, and you can investigate that. It depends on your goals.

LAUNCH: Finally, launch! Launching your book doesn't have to be super difficult, and depending on the purpose of the book, you can decide how much time you want to put into promoting it. You will need to promote it, but make sure that the promotion time fits your needs.

Some possible goals for a book:
>   A. Getting more clients.
>   B. Getting speaking engagements.
>   C. Building credibility in your industry.
>   D. Building an alternate revenue stream.
>   F. Building part of your sales funnel.

Your goals for the book will shape its content. Determine how you will be using this book as your "calling card" and create a book that fits those needs. Here are some examples.

A. Getting more clients

For many of us, just getting more clients and using our book as a great way to introduce our business is the main reason for creating a book. I did that with my first two books: Choosing a Caregiver, and Leadership Girl. Both helped me get more clients and put information out there that is of value to my clients. It has also given them a way to get to know me, in perhaps a way that they might not otherwise.

B. Getting Speaking Engagements

If you've ever entertained the thought of becoming a speaker, or using speaking engagements as part of your business, then having a book can be a great way to open those doors. As a bonus, many times you will get the opportunity to sell your book in the back of the room or in the lobby. You can sometimes negotiate a deal to have the sponsoring organization purchase copies of the book to give to each of the attendees. This could pay your speaking fees without having to pay you directly, so the book is a great tool for speaking engagements.

C. Building Credibility in Your Industry

Nothing says credibility like having written the book on the subject. If you want that instant mark and recognition that you know what you're doing, and are an established leader in your field, this can be just the ticket to get there. People will respect you more for having your words in print.

D. Building an Alternate Revenue Stream

Selling books can be a healthy additional revenue stream in your business. However, I have talked to a lot of authors who expect their book to go instantly viral when it's released. They also have the expectation that they will make boodles of cash by selling a single book. For most authors, unless you take a significant amount of time to promote the book, and have written several books, or already have a national presence, the book is not necessarily going to be a significant source of revenue.

If you intend to make money from a book, please know that for the vast majority of authors, books aren't necessarily a huge revenue stream in-and-of themselves. They are tools.

E. Building Part of Your Sales Funnel

A book can be a great part of the lower cost options for a sales funnel. Many people will offer a digital copy of their book for free, or they will offer it free with shipping. It can also be a great way to advertise your business, by sending people to your website, for an additional offer, or even a workbook, as part of the book.

It can help you build an audience and build trust in a way that other parts of a funnel might not do. When it becomes a formal part of a sales funnel, it can be leveraged on a massive scale.

Imagine getting a free copy of a best seller when you sign up for someone's email list. Or what about buying a great book that your friends are recommending, and then seeing that it offers a complimentary workbook, for free, that you can only get on the author's website?

It can be a fabulous way to bring in dozens of other clients.

Choosing a Publisher

Publishing a book today is not the same thing as it used to be. In the past, you would submit your book to a variety of publishers, and then negotiate a deal to get paid when they publish your book.

That still happens, but it's increasingly rare. Many traditional publishers want to know the size of your email list and social media following, because they want a guarantee that your fame will sell books. And, frankly, if you're not nationally recognized, you probably won't get an offer from a big publishing house.

Instead, most people now go to someone who has experience formatting their book, and then end up self-publishing the book on KDP and CreateSpace, for a nominal fee.

Some publishers, book coaches, and formatters charge a large amount, and can "guarantee" best seller status. Not all those means pan out. Some charge a large fee, but don't guarantee success. Determine how you'll be using your book before deciding to spend big bucks. You can always choose the less expensive route. There is no set manner to publishing these days. Figure out the best way that meets your needs and do it.

Remember, your book is your $5 calling card. It will give you credibility, help you gain clients, and introduce you and your business to others.

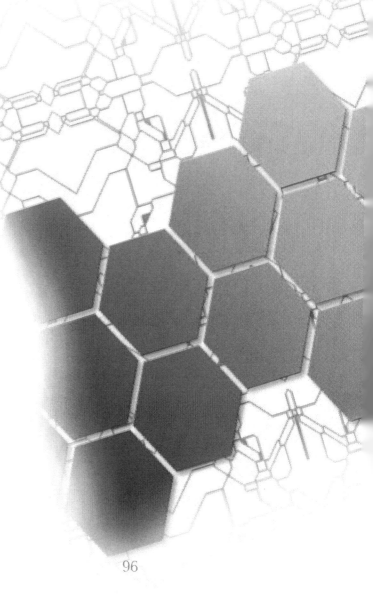

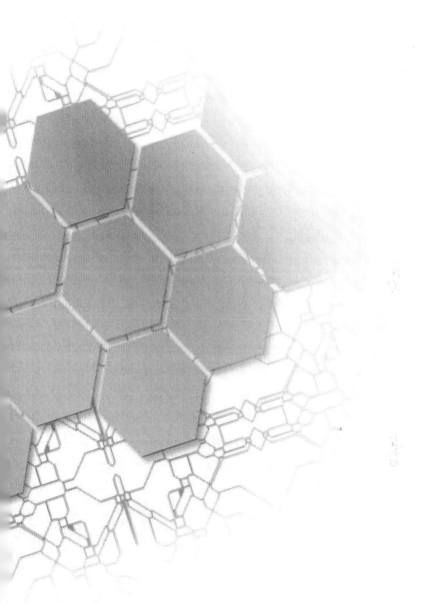

7. Be the Go-To Connector

"The people with the
truest connections
and relationships
came out ahead.."

7. Be the Go-To Connector

If you want to get lots and lots of clients, become someone that gives back. It is known as the giver's gain.

The idea is that you connect people who need specific resources. If you have a list of accountants, bookkeepers, printers, realtors, and all kinds of professionals, you can easily set yourself up to become the go-to connector in your network.

It can be an incredibly powerful way to get referrals back as well. The idea is that many people will reciprocate if you give them referrals. You can test out the idea by sending a couple of test referrals to a possible partner, and depending on how well they handle the client, and whether they refer someone back to you, will determine whether you keep referring to them or not.

When I was at Duke, studying for my MBA, one of the things we did was a case study to understand who connectors are in the network. We sat down, and made a list of connections, and their connections to each other. There is software that will do this.

The people with the truest connections and relationships came out ahead.

If you want to be a connector, there are a few things you can do to get to that status, including getting out and meeting people. When you do these things, keep in mind that you want to build real, honest relationships with people.

• **Go to networking meetings.** The key to networking meetings is to schedule 1:1 meetings with attendees afterwards. I learned that the weekly or monthly regular meeting is essentially a dog and pony show. The real business happens outside of the meeting itself, while the meeting itself is there to bring more people in to join the network. Go out for a drink or coffee, meet for a meal with other members, and THERE is where you will find real business taking place.

• **Join a social network or two.** Sometimes the social networks will yield the most authentic connections. Many cities have them. In Raleigh we have our City Club. It's a skyrise members-only venue with access to private office spaces, conference rooms, concierge business services, plus a bar and restaurant, providing a calendar full of events and social opportunities. These clubs are places where you can go and meet people, join various interest groups, and networking groups, and meet lots of possible connections for your business. I have met and made some amazing contacts through this network, and when I work it, it does wonders for me. When I don't? Well, the results aren't so stellar either. It's all about working the groups that you're in.

"If you want to get lots and lots of clients, become someone that gives back "

• **Volunteer for a cause you believe in.** It doesn't even have to be directly connected to your business, but the relationships you build will be worth a lifetime of referrals, and connections. As a Girl Scout leader for 15 years now, I've been able to build relationships that will last me a lifetime. Many of my girls have been all the way through high school and are in college. My co-leaders have become life-long friends. I love that the parents have supported me in my business and have referred to me to their friends.

• **Join a religious community.** Find a group that shares your faith. Many religious groups (though certainly not all) offer networking groups to support their members. Hope Community Church here in Raleigh has a massive congregation, with many satellite campuses, and groups of job seekers. Several of the Baptist Churches have mentoring programs around job seeking, and small business owners. I know that this isn't something that my church particularly offers or supports, but it is out there in some places, if it's your thing.

• **Talk to random strangers.** Yep. Too often we just don't talk to people. I go to the YMCA and have had some amazing conversations with the other people there. Over time, we build relationships. It's especially true with places you visit often.

• **Connect to people on social media, including LinkedIn, Facebook, Twitter, etc.** I made some long-time friends through BabyCenter when I was pregnant with my children. I am still in contact with many of those women today, and some of them have become my strongest support network.

Network: Work It Like You Mean It

Now, I'm guessing you are going to think that I'm a natural connector, and extrovert here, and that I love going to networking meetings.

I must confess here that I'm actually an introvert, and that connecting with people, and going to networking meetings is not something that I naturally do. These are all skills that I've learned over time.

A few years ago, when I started learning how to network, one of my sales people would poke fun at me, because I was so hopeless going into a room with a fairly large number of people in it. I would walk into the room, and freeze. Terrified. Then I would work my way out of the terror and start talking to maybe one or two people for the entire time. I couldn't work a room, or even work my way around the room. It was funny and not funny at the same time.

Slowly, I developed my skills for small talk, and connecting with people. For those of us who are awkward, introverted, engineering types, we must practice and playact our social interactions and chit chatting. Working a room is something that does not come naturally. It can take years to develop, but it's possible.

Want to give your 60-second presentation? It took several coaches working me over, and helping me write out my speech, and then memorizing it, and practicing, until I could deliver without seeming like I had it memorized. Yes. Memorizing it, and then learning to deliver it without sounding totally memorized.

I started visiting various networking groups, until I found a group that I fit into, and was comfortable with. Since this is a business activity, it was important to me to get actual referrals, and business out of the deal, not just make friends. I had to join several groups over periods of time, and ultimately settled on a couple of groups where I got the most referrals. And, that's key: if you're not getting referrals, it's not a networking group. Keep trying until you find a networking group where you help others and they help you. Otherwise, it's a waste of time.

Finding a good group and connecting with the group isn't easy. I have found plenty of groups where I love the people but was unable to get much business. I ended up leaving those groups for more productive groups, but I've stayed in touch, and still support many of my friends from those groups. Don't give up the people, give up the group.

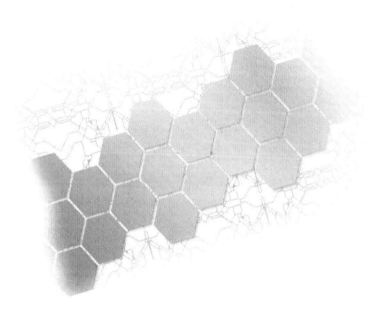

Your 8-Figure Business Blueprint

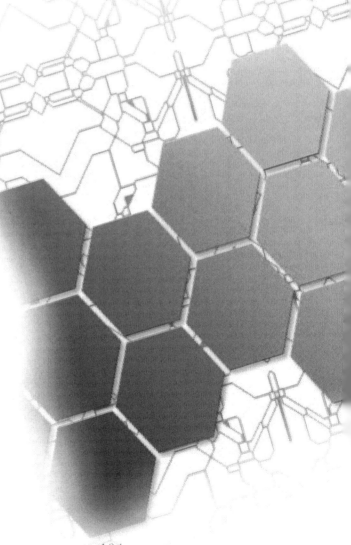

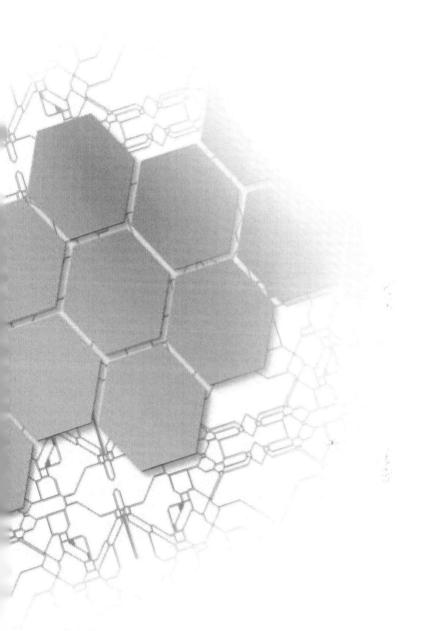

8. Weaving a Presence: Websites

"For many people, their website is the cornerstone of their marketing efforts."

8. Weaving a Presence: Websites

For many people, their website is the corner-stone of their marketing efforts. I can't tell you how many people have the mistaken notion that they can put up their website, and that they won't really have to do any other marketing, because people will just find them.

It's disappointing to me, because some digital marketing experts oversell what a website will do for your business, and overcharge for what it will do for your business. They also encourage people to overspend, because it obviously lines their pockets.

The real scoop is that a good website can help you get more clients because people are more likely to be able to find you online. Websites are not, however, things that exist in isolation. They are not antidotes for your marketing ills. You don't even need a website to get lots of clients.

Don't believe me?
If you want to sell crafts online, you can use eBay, Etsy, or Amazon. They all have built in SEO.

If you're an attorney? A business listing on Google, and a Facebook page are enough to start out.

If you're an accountant worth your salt, you will get referrals through word of mouth. Most CPAs stay very, very busy, even without a website.

That said, a website can be a great calling card for the world.

Think about it this way: your business is like a wagon, and each marketing technique is like one of the Budweiser Clydesdales. You need several of those big, critters to pull your wagon. If they aren't harnessed, and pulling all together, then your wagon isn't going to go anywhere, unless you happen to get lucky and roll downhill.

Your website is like one of those Clydesdales. When you work with the website, and other marketing techniques, you are likely to start generating lots of great clients.

So, what should you really put on your website?
1. List of Services
2. Contact Information and Location (if warranted)
3. Any Information for Selling Your Services.

Optional pieces:
1. Blog
2. Videos
3. Picture Galleries

I see businesses that really struggle with the entire website thing, and who put more time and energy into a website than they will receive back. That is a shame. The website is a tool for your business and should be working for you. The trick is to develop a presence that represents your business brand well, is updated and maintained regularly, and contains accurate, current information.

Or course, it's important that it be visually pleasing, but it also needs to be easy to use. It should also be easy for prospects to find the information they want.

Technical stuff you need to know:

When you're developing your website, you should ask questions about where the website will be hosted, and by whom. You also need to ask who will own the content.

Many website developers will insist on hosting your website themselves, which can be great, or it can be risky. I've seen too many cases of people getting out of the web development business which leaves their clients in a lurch and puts their websites at risk. It also means that they must move their websites with almost no notice, which can be prohibitively costly.

The second question you should ask is to determine who owns the content on your website. Some developers will hold websites hostage, and it can be difficult or impossible to get access to your site, and your content. You should always own your own content.

When you first start your business, and are having your first website built, be sure it's supportable. I'm a big believer in making sure that whatever you do, it should be totally maintainable, whether it's by you, or someone else.

I really love using Wordpress, because it's easy to maintain, change and update. It's also easy to find someone who can step in and fix whatever problems you have because nearly everyone in the industry knows Wordpress. My preferred platform is Wordpress with the host being Siteground.

You can register your domain through Siteground and get exceptional customer service help if you need it.

Website Content

Sadly, I can't just wave a magic wand and create content on a website. I really, truly wish I could. But I can't.

When I ask clients for information on their business, it's because, as good as I am, I'm not a mind reader. I can't create something from nothing. If I don't have content, neither will your website.

So, if you want a good product, you're going to need to answer questions, and take part in the planning of content for your website. If you are a small business owner, that may mean biographies, stories about how the business started, and more. Those are the types of things, I can't just pull out of thin air. You'll need to formulate your story and cast your vision.

Expect to write some of the content or copy on your website to make sure that it reflects your business, and your tone. In addition, you can hire a writer to craft and/or an editor to clean-up your copy, but you'll still have to oversee the content to make sure it says what you want it to say. Don't expect to sit back and let professionals "take over." Be present and involved in the process.

Your 8-Figure Business Blueprint

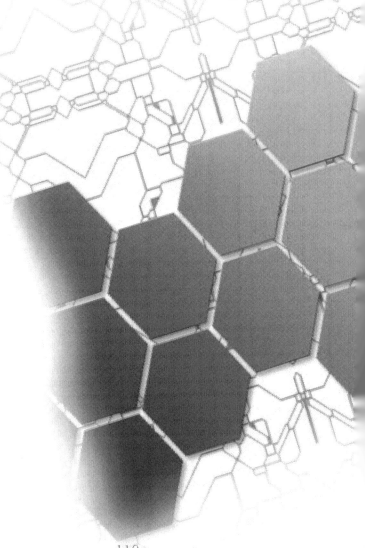

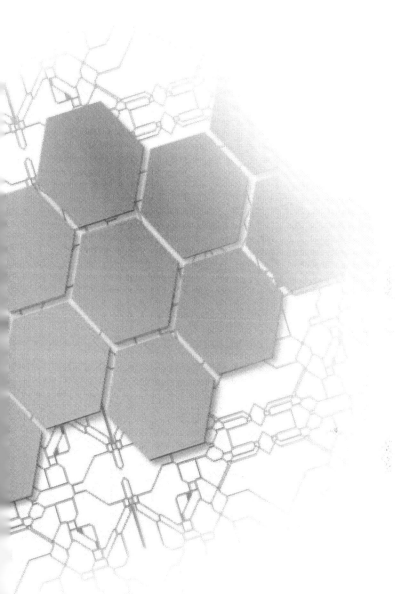

9. Filling the Pipe: Sales Funnels

"They think that it
must be something
super sophisticated."

9. Filling the Pipe: Sales Funnels

The idea of a sales funnel strikes absolute terror into the heart of many small business owners. They think that it must be something super sophisticated.

In fact, in the online world, some sales funnels cost tens of thousands of dollars and are incredibly complicated, but some aren't. There are lots of different kinds of sales funnels, that work different kinds of ways, and some are much simpler than others.

How do they work? A sales funnel is a diagrammatic representation of the process. You want to have people become aware of your business and products by following a specific set of steps on the way to becoming a client. They go through various methods to get there: emails, social media, texts, landing pages, and more landing pages.

Entire books have been written on sales funnels, so if you want to become an expert, just read more about it. Basically, it's taking someone from Awareness, to Interest, to Decision, and then finally to Action.

Your funnel can be as simple or as complex as you like, and there are lots of different types of software for building a funnel. Ontraport, to Leadpages are two more complex systems. Wordpress gives you simple landing pages. And, there are many more. The limits are only defined by your own imagination and budget.

We frequently set up funnels for our clients, but it's about figuring out what the right type of funnel is for each individual business owner, based on their business, budget and needs. The costs don't have to be astronomical.

Different Kinds of Funnels

1. Free opt in to upsell - In this type of funnel, you offer people something of value for free in exchange for their email addresses. Once you have their email address, you offer something for sale, then more and different items for sale.

2. Webinar to a call - Many people will run a webinar to a sales call. Usually, something that the customer is interested in is offered on the webinar. The webinar can either be live, or it can be recorded, and automated.

3. Facebook group or online community to a call - An online community can serve as a free or low cost funnel, if you focus on engagement with your prospects.

4. Ads to a landing page to make a call - One of the simplest sales funnels is just running ads to drive people to a simple landing page, with a call to action of making a phone call, or filling in a form, to learn more about a product or service.

5. Newsletters - so often business owners neglect their email lists. When you have people who have already been clients or customers, if you market to them again, they are more likely to return as clients.

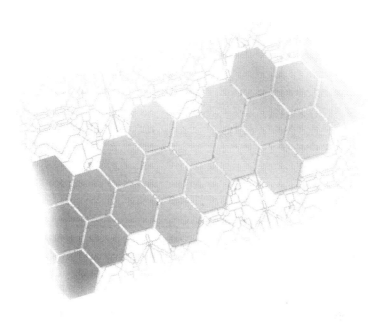

FEARLESS MARKETING

Your 8-Figure Business Blueprint

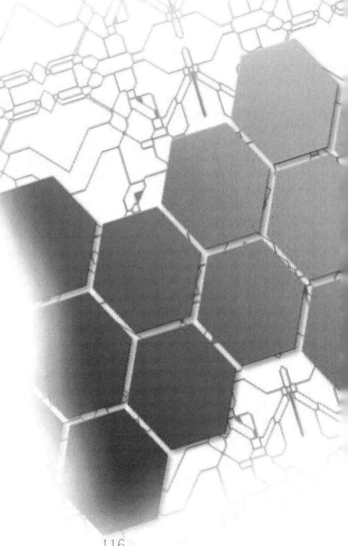

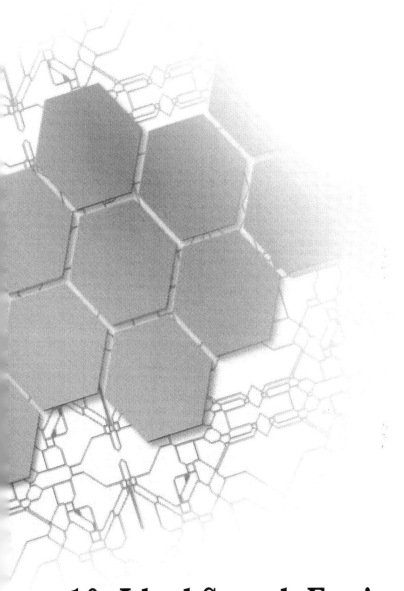

10. Ideal Search Engine Optimization

"The mythical unicorn of getting your website to show up ahead of your competition."

10. Ideal Search Engine Optimization

There are a lot of things that you can do to drive more traffic to your website and bring more eyeballs to your products or services. The mythical unicorn of getting your website to show up ahead of your competition, and the increased business you're going to get because of being first is called search engine optimization, or SEO.

Truth is: SEO is a process, it is always evolving, and it is not an overnight success story that will magically happen for your website.

By focusing on search engine optimization, you can let the search engines, like Google know that you exist. When they know you exist, they send increased traffic to your site. Good behavior yields more traffic.

At a basic level, it includes two main sets of components:
    1. **Onsite**- SEO
    2. **Offsite**- SEO

The search engines, like Google, look at a large variety of different parameters to decide how to rank a page more highly. The algorithms constantly change, on nearly a daily basis. They constantly evolve and switch parameters.

There have been lots of strategies over the years that people have used to try to game the search engines, like keyword stuffing, and other techniques. Keyword stuffing is a black hat technique where keywords are loaded into a website's background. It's highly suspect. Keyword stuffing, along with other sketchy techniques, do not result in the best possible content getting ranked most highly. To manage this, Google, and other search engines, have been working to stop the shenanigans and close the loop so that the best content gets the most attention, not just the one scamming the system.

A lot of people spend too much time and too much money trying to improve their SEO. But playing games means you must keep playing different games as the rules change. What it comes down to is this: your SEO is about ensuring your website is packed with high quality content and provides a great experience for users. If you focus on quality over "gaming the system," then you're more likely to rank highly on the search engines.

1. Onsite SEO

Onsite SEO comprises of a variety of different components and can be facilitated by using a variety of different tools. My favorite tool, and probably the most common tool is Yoast SEO. They offer a free and a paid version of the tool.

When you create onsite SEO, there are a few different things you focus on:

1. Quality of the Content - The content should be as high quality as possible. Quality is measured by things like readability, backlinks and links between content.

2. Meta Tags - Make sure that you fill out the meta tags and descriptions on your website. If you don't fill these out, Google will automatically fill them in, and you may not get the results you're looking for. So, what exactly IS a Meta description or meta tag? This is the description that google shows on the search page, when your page shows up. It is always better if you can decide exactly what shows up about your website, rather than leaving it to chance.

3. Cornerstone Content - Decide which content on your site is the "most important" content, and focus on having more articles, and pages link to that content. Obviously, you can't be everything to everyone, so trying to rank highly for a bunch of different topics may not be to your benefit. Instead, try focusing on a very narrow set of topics on your page, and have the pages not only linking to one another, but also having similar topics.

3. Internal Linking - Link to other pages within your website. By doing this, you let search engines know what pages go together. By including a few links on each page, you also give people a little nudge to help them stay around on your website for a bit longer, which also can help your SEO.

4. External Linking - Links to other websites, can improve your SEO. I know that this sounds weird, but it's true. By making sure to be a good team player, and that you connect to other websites, you improve your own SEO, and that of the other websites as well.

5. Google Analytics - Installing and utilizing Google Analytics can help tell you what is going on with your website. It also tells Google that you're serious about your SEO, and your analytics. It gives you a little bump in your SEO, just by having it installed and configured. Go figure.

7. Bounce Rates and Time on Site - The bounce rate for your website is the number of people who come onto the website, then bounce back off, or leave before going to another page. Google measures how many pages people visit on your site, bounce rate, and how long they spend on your site. Those metrics all go together for the search engine to decide just how good the content is on your website. The longer that people stay, on average, the better.

8. Long Tail Keywords - Keywords are what we use to tell Google your page is about, and we optimize the content on a particular page around a certain word, or group of words. The reality is that it can be incredibly hard to rank or get yourself found for a keyword like "realtor," because there are hundreds of thousands of other realtors out there, along with a major website, called realtor.com. Instead, it's typically better to go after long tail keywords that relate to your topic, which would be something like "Raleigh realtor," or "real estate in Raleigh," etc. The more of these phrases that you target, the more that you signal the search engines that you are providing a certain type of content. That means that yes, you end up writing a variety of different articles about topics that pertain to similar long tail keywords but are on different aspects of those keywords. One example of this is writing about different neighborhoods, or even different things to do in the area.

9. Comments on Your Blog - Good comments, high quality comments, and lots of interaction on your blog and website is something that the search engine gods want to see lots of. The more of it you have, the better. The challenge? Getting people to comment and leave meaningful comments that are better than a "good job," so that you can generate lively conversations.

Note that you don't have to do all the work yourself, but you should be aware of what's going on. Especially before you pull out your wallet and hand over your hard-earned cash to someone who says that they know what they're doing for search engine optimization. Not everyone is an expert.

2. Offsite SEO

Offsite SEO is anything that doesn't directly happen on your website, and can be every bit as important, if not more so than what you do on your website to try to improve SEO. It can also be the harder part of doing SEO for your site.

1. Backlinks - One of the strongest ways that you can signal your page authority to search engines is by having high quality backlinks to your site. That means that other sites are linking to you as a source of more information, and giving you more authority. It can be somewhat tricky to build these backlinks, but that is what a reputable SEO agency will do for you. They will help create high quality articles that will include a backlink to your company and submit them to other websites.

2. Social Media - Social Media has even gotten into the act for search engine optimization. Google has started measuring engagement on social media for links that link back to your site. The more your links are followed, shared, liked, retweeted, and generally acknowledged, the better that the search engines like your social media.

What NOT to do for SEO

There are plenty of things that you are probably thinking of right now that are not a good idea when it comes to improving your site's SEO. Some of them might or might not get you into trouble with the search engine gods, and some of them will get your site blacklisted faster than you can blink.

Unfortunately, the list of exactly what will get you into hot water changes regularly, even more regularly than my 11-year-old son changes his socks.

The lesson to take away from this is that you need to focus on providing high quality content, as well as building your website and links in a way that are smart, ethical and not "weird" or "unnatural."

Here are some of my favorite things that will land you on the dark side:

1. Keyword stuffing. Google is looking for natural language. It used to be that they looked for a lot of occurrences of a keyword on a page to rank highly, so people would write copy for their website that included lots (and I mean, lots and lots!) of instances of the desired or target word. They would also hide the word in the background of the page, where computers could read it, but human eyes could not. This practice is known as keyword stuffing, and it will land you on Google's blacklist nowadays. So, don't do it.

2. Directory Linking. Some people figured out that the number of backlinks to a website was important, so they started coming up with different and creative ways to build those backlinks without having to do much work. One of those was to create a multitude of online directories of links, like Yahoo, Bing, or Google, but without nearly as much value. They are simply lists of links. The big search engines figured this out and have started blacklisting anyone detected doing this.

3. Links in Comments. A link is a link, right? Well, some inventive people figured out that leaving comments on other people's blogs, with a link back to your own website counts as a link. Or rather it did. Now, Google and other search engines have figured out this scam, and they now ignore links in comments on blogs. Leaving comments is a nice thing to do on other people's blogs. But leaving comments for the sake of a link? It doesn't work so well anymore.

You probably get the idea. Anything you to do try to "game the system" is likely to run you afoul of the search engines. And, that's an unhealthy place to find yourself.

Be especially wary of anyone who tells you that they can do this instantaneously, or who says they can guarantee that you'll get on the first page of Google within a certain timeframe, or that you'll be listed first. Unfortunately, there are no real ways to guarantee placement, or that you'll see a huge bump in where you are found on SEO on your website. The only thing a good SEO manager can offer is that you will see a steady improvement over time.

Your 8-Figure Business Blueprint

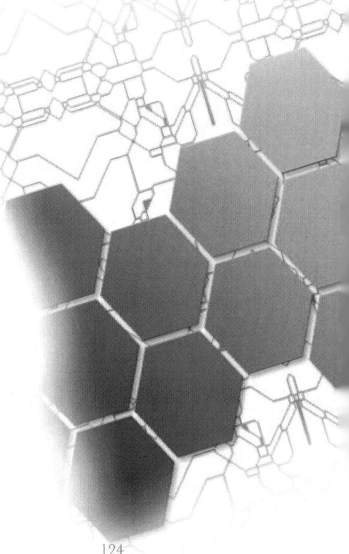

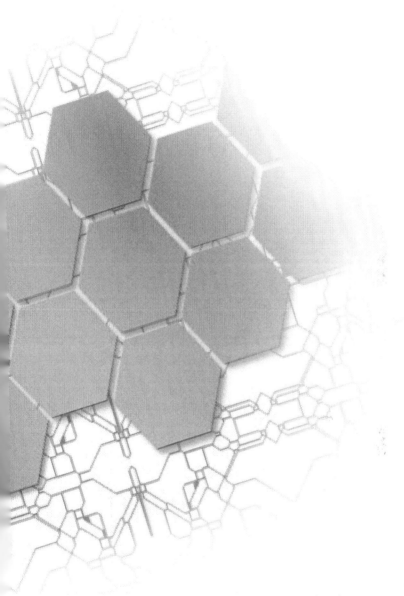

11. Paid Advertising: Boom or Bust?

"It seems a multiplier:
you put money in and out
comes more money."

11. Paid Advertising: Boom or Bust?

It can be tempting when you talk to someone from Yelp to hear the siren's call of buying ads. It seems a multiplier: you put money in and out comes more money. Super easy, right? Unfortunately, the results aren't always there for many small businesses, which can be super frustrating.

One of my clients has had several different advertising agencies calling him, hounding him for months to just TRY their service. Of course, he wants more business, and they keep telling him how much more business he's going to get from their paid ads.

After probably three to four months of nagging and hounding, he finally gave in and paid a few hundred dollars a month for ads. Ads that didn't work. He was completely frustrated with such a complete waste of time and money.

Now, I do want to be clear, paid ads, done well, DO provide a return on investment. Sometimes a huge return on investment. And other times? Unfortunately, paid ads don't give always give a good bang for a buck, and here's why: Targeting.

Targeting is the most critical part of understanding and predicting whether ads will work in the first place. If you are a business owner in Raleigh, chances are, advertising to people in Durham, which is 20 miles away, is going to be a waste of your time and money. Most of your client base is going to come from a narrow radius of your office. Instead, focus your ads, on a narrower area, to the types of people who are more likely to become your clients.

The beauty of using Facebook Ads, and Google PPC is that they allow you to focus your ads on the exact types of people you think would make great clients, and not the entire world. That means that you are using wording that your ideal clients use when looking for you. It also gets you in front of them when they search for your type of business.

Have you ever had the experience of searching for a product or service online? Perhaps you were interested in a certain type of car, so you searched for it. And, suddenly that car is all over your social media feeds? It's kinda cool, and kinda creepy at the same time. What's going on is something called retargeting.

Retargeting happens when a code, or sometimes called a pixel, is loaded onto your website. This code doesn't affect your website performance, and visitors can't see it's there. When a new visitor comes to your site, the code drops a browser cookie into their browser. These are "cookies." As those same visitors browse the Web, your cookie alerts your retargeting provider to know it's time to offer these people your ads. This makes sure that your ads are provided people who have previously visited your site and have shown interest in your products or services. This is how retargeting works, provided you are using a reputable company, or managing the ads for yourself.

Successful ads hinge on a few different components: targeting; creative component, which is made up of the images, pictures, and look and feel; copy, which is the written content; and, marketing. If any one of those components falls apart, then you will notice that your ads aren't nearly as effective. In fact, they may not even work at all.

Where can you advertise?

There are lots of different venues for paid ads for your business. Other than the obvious Internet sites, the list also includes radio, TV, magazines, billboards, flyers, mailers and more. There is almost no end to places that you can advertise your business.

Which of these is going to work for you depends on the exact nature of your business. I think that if you are going to engage in these types of ads, you need to pay for an additional tracking phone number through a company specializing in phone call tracking, like CallRail. You post that tracking phone number on your ad and then your company measures the results.

When you use tracking phone numbers, use a different number for each place you advertise, whether it's Facebook ads, your website, magazines, radio, or any other locations for advertising your business. Measuring the return on investment, so that you can tell what is working and what it not, is super important to knowing where to spend your money.

Too often we don't measure our ROI, return on investment, and just assume that since we see an increase in the number of clients, that it's working. But, there's no correlation if there's no data. Precise tracking will help you determine which ads gain you business, and which ones don't.

Questions you should ask before advertising

When you are contemplating running ads in a magazine, on the radio, with banners or signs, or in other places, you should determine the audience reach and demographics. I pointed out above that not having the right targeting, and the right audience, could mean that you don't see a return on investment for your advertising dollars.

Here are some questions you should ask any advertising company before paying for ads or campaigns:

- What is your target demographic? Who is going to hear, or see this ad?
- What is your reach? How many people are going to see this ad?
- What is your experience with other people like me?
- How many of my competitors are you also advertising?
- How long have you been doing this?
- Do you create the graphics, ad, creative, or do we?
- How long does it take to get started?
- What is the overall cost? What is the cost per impression?
- Can you guarantee that a certain number of people will see this ad?
- Please show me numbers for other people who have advertised with you in the past.
- Can you give me references for other companies you have worked with in the past?

Back Away from the Boost Button

Facebook makes it incredibly easy to boost your post. In most cases, that is just like handing them your debit card, and telling them to just take your money for fun and games.

Regrettably, I have done it plenty of times myself.

What I have learned is that you need to have a clear call to action on every ad that you run, and a clear reason to do it. Brand recognition is lovely, but unless you're a huge company, it doesn't do you a lot of good, or make you money.

For instance, big advertisers like Pepsi or Coors pay millions to get their brands in front of audiences. They sponsor sporting events and concerts. Their logos appears everywhere, on cups, banners, cars, billboards, tickets, menus, you name it, it's there. People have already bought into their product. They're going to drink a Pepsi or Coors because they know it, and they've had it. They don't have to convince their market to try this new thing called a Coors beer or a Pepsi soda. They must simply remind people of their brand.

This isn't true for the average business. Maybe you're a lawyer or dentist. You don't have to convince someone they need help with a traffic ticket or a filling. They know that. They just don't know YOU. Your logo or brand isn't going to bring them in, but your ad will.

Brand recognition works best if you're a national or regional brand, so they can spend millions on ads just to promote their image. All others need results from their ads; meaning, they need clients brought into their businesses because of those ads.

Boosting, while an easy click of the button on Facebook, doesn't necessarily allow you to target, and set the same parameters, which are things you can do with a regular ad campaign. That means loss of control over what you're doing. It scattered, not targeted.

Instead, focus on doing something with a clear call to action, and clear strategy. Once you have the correct pieces in place, ads are much more likely to be profitable for you.

What about running campaigns for "likes?"

There is this wonderful misconception that "likes" on a page somehow turn into dollars.

When I first started my business, I did campaigns to increase the number of "likes" on my page. Great. Lots of people "liked" my page. No one bought.

What I quickly learned through my experience is that "likes" are nice, and sort of ego-boosting, but they don't necessarily translate into sales. You're much more likely to get relevant "likes" on your page if you are posting content that people enjoy.

What you must do it simultaneously run ad campaigns. You've captured your audience, now reel them in as clients by advertising to them. Get them to click on ads that go directly to your website, or give a call to action such as having them call you or email you for an appointment.

So, while people are coming to your Facebook page to appreciate your postings, they will also see your ads.

"Likes" are nothing but a vanity number on a page, and Facebook in particular has made it harder to tell how many "likes" a page actually has. Paying for campaigns just to get more "likes" on your page isn't likely to get you the results you're hoping for.

Your 8-Figure Business Blueprint

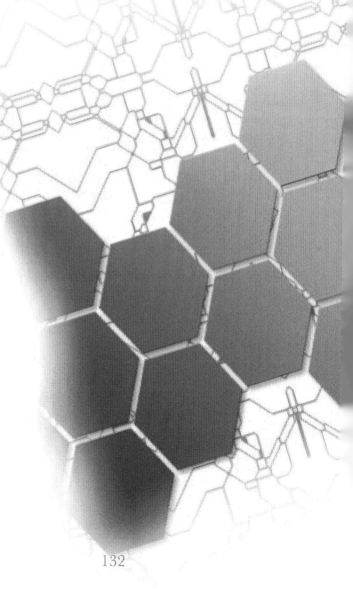

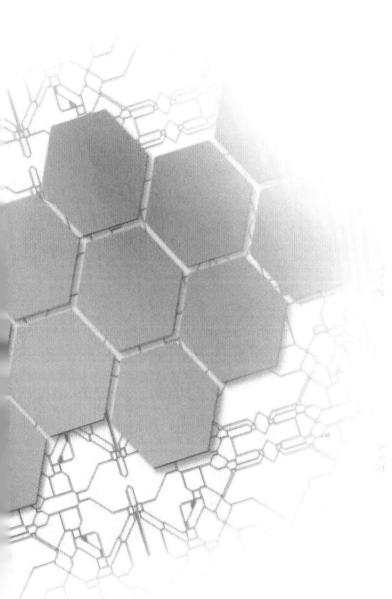

12. Social Media Done Right

"I regularly get asked which platform is best for business."

12. Social Media Done Right

The sheer number of social media platforms has exploded over the last few years, and there are social media platforms for every single demographic. As someone who does a lot of work on a variety of different social media platforms, I regularly get asked which platform is best for business, and my answer is a non-committal, **"it depends."**

I'm serious. It really does depend on which platforms resonate the most with you, and where you can envision spending time. I recommend starting with one, or maybe two, social media platforms in the beginning. That is, unless you have someone dedicated to running your social media accounts full time. Because social media, no matter the platform, can be a huge time-suck.

You might be wondering if you can just have someone on your admin staff do this. Well, that can work, but frequently it doesn't. I've seen it fail more times than I care to count. Unless you have someone who is extremely social media savvy, it will take them many hours to do the work, and they won't do it particularly well. That may mean that you end up spending a lot more money for less results. Which is not very much fun.

My recommendation is to choose a platform you like, and one you can maintain initially, before calling in a professional. Once you've had some success, you can then afford to hire someone to do it on your behalf.

Each platform has its own quirks, and they are constantly updating rules about how you can post, where, when, sharing, and formatting. I have found that keeping up with the updates on various social media platforms is nearly as intense as keeping up with all the changes on Google's search engines. Since none of the platforms really tell you what they're doing, or when they're going to do it, staying current with all of it can be a bit of a challenge.

I only accept connection requests from my real friends

I hear from people that they only accept Facebook friend requests from people who are their "real" friends, no business connections. I hear this sentiment a LOT.

The reality is that all things being equal, people only do business with those they know, like, and trust. Remember that: KNOW, LIKE and TRUST. Those are the keys to being the go-to provider. They'll do business with you if they know you, if they like you, and they trust you.

One of the best ways to stay in front of business acquaintances is via social media. That means connecting with them at every opportunity.

One of those occasions to stay in front of people and connect regularly is via social media. The people I know who do the best in their business are the ones who use their social media as an extension of themselves. They also connect with a broad section of people on their social media. They post things that are interesting, funny, witty, and appropriate for their business colleagues to know about them.

It makes them more human, more relatable, in a way that makes people want to do business with them. It's a win-win all the way around.

A word of caution: stay away from divisive issues and angry tones. Much of social media is filled with hit-pieces, slanderous articles, anger-provoking sentiments, lies, half-truths, misquotes and dubious information meant to stir-up emotions and outrage. This is not for you, so stay clear of those things.

There are three topics they tell you never to talk about in professional setting: religion, sex and politics. Let that bleed over to your Facebook profile, as well. The only deviation would be if religion were part of your personal or business identity and people might appreciate you more or seek you out based on your religious leanings.

Make sure that you get rid of the stupid stuff you've posted previously, too. Comb through your posts and tweets to see what you've posted in the past.

You may want to permanently delete what could be considered offensive material.

Going forward, post funny memes, cute sayings, inspirational quotes, helpful information, local events, etc. Also, pub your networking partners, other small businesses, and the like. Helping others is a good thing. What goes around, comes around. Remember, people will perceive your heart based on what you post. Let's bring the fun back to social media and keep away from the negativity.

But, you say, I don't want personal information to get out about my family. Well, guess what? We live in an age where there is only perceived privacy. With an Internet connection, a laptop, and a bit of skill, anyone can know just about anything about you. It's all out there for the finding.

You can veil your kids—not posting detailed photos or information, using cute nicknames for them, and the like, if you want a semblance of privacy. But, remember, people do business with people they know, like and trust. If you're so veiled that people don't "know" you, then your profile isn't helpful.

When you think of your social media, it's time to start accepting connections from colleagues and staying positive, while stop putting up stupid stuff on your social media.

Tools

There are some amazing tools out there that can help you maintain your social media platforms. These tools can help you focus on creating content in batches, setting up your posting schedule, and monitoring any responses that you might be getting on social media.

You don't have to post at the exact moment in time you want it to appear. You can delay posts and schedule them in advance. This saves you from remembering to manage your accounts every day.

You can create gorgeous, professional looking posts, too. You can post simultaneously to all your platforms at once. And, a plethora of other, great functions.

Tools really are the key to staying sane when it comes to managing social media platforms, and they are the insider's secret that you need.

Here are some of my favorite tools for managing social media:

1. Canva - Canva is a beautiful tool that allows you to create graphics for your social media for free, or a nominal cost. It allows simple drag and drop functionality, access to many fonts, colors, and graphics. That means you can create professional-looking graphics for your business in a matter of a few minutes. The best part is that you can create graphics in bunches, or batches, so you can do quite a few in a small amount of time, then download them, and schedule them. You may have heard to use different graphics for Pinterest to see what sticks. Here's how you can do that successfully without wanting to pull your hair out.

2. Pixabay and Pexels - Pixabay.com and Pexels.com are two websites that you can use online to download free graphics, photos, and images for your social media, website, and more. It is super important that you get your images from a known good location, and that you have the proper rights in place to use images. Otherwise, you could be hit by a lawsuit for thousands of dollars for using someone else's images.

3. Buffer - Buffer is one of my favorite platforms for scheduling content on social media. For $10/month or $102 for an entire year, you can schedule content to your heart's content on up to 10 different social media accounts.

4. Tailwind - Tailwind was really created for scheduling pins on Pinterest. In it, you can join tribes, and create your own tribe, and pin from there. It allows you to pin to multiple boards, at the same time, and is easy to use overall. If you are going to use Pinterest to drive traffic to your blog, this is a great tool.

Facebook

Facebook has become the 800-pound gorilla in the social media world, for good reason. They have a huge focus on customer experience, and on making money off advertising revenue. If you can stay on Facebook's good side, then you will do well. And, you can make some decent money from utilizing it.

Generally, you should focus on posting regularly, and on having good inter-action on your posts. You must post things that people want to interact with, not just sell, sell, sell. Yes, I know you want to sell, but to get seen, you must get creative about the whole promotion thing. Since today's audiences are immune to ads, and super used to fast forwarding past any ads, you're going to have to get creative about posting, and getting seen.

A word about selling: if you are always "selling" through your posts, you'll turn people off to your message. They'll block you, or snooze you, or worse: they'll "unlike" your page or unfriend you. You want to keep them capti-vated and motivated, not saturated with your sales pitch. You may be very excited about your sales message, your promotions, and your offerings. But, not everyone is, so tone down the selling which can come across as needy and greedy.

There are a lot of myths and misconceptions about the platform, and it's also super important to understand the terms and conditions of the platform as well.

1. Facebook's terms and conditions dictate that your personal page is for personal stuff only and shouldn't be named after your business. You also only get one account per person. So, you can't have a Facebook account for friends and family, and one for professional connections. It doesn't work that way. If Facebook decides you have violated its terms, or just suspects you might have, it will have your account shut right down. Not pretty. So, keep your personal page for fun stuff.

2. "Likes" don't mean squat. Sorry to put this out there, but "likes" on your business page don't mean anything, really. There might be some vague cor-relation between "likes" on your page, and size of your business, but "likes" don't always translate into buyers. You can't buy groceries or pay rent with "likes."

3. The normal rules that apply to friendships and relationships also apply online. So, if you wouldn't say something to someone's face, it has no place online. If you are trying to market your business, the same reasoning goes. Messaging people you aren't connected with will get your account reported and shut down before you can even blink.

4. Please make sure that you update your profile to reflect your business and

point to your business page. Posting that you are "self-employed" does not help anyone find your business. I guarantee people are going to meet you, look up your social media profile, then try to find your business. If you don't make it easy for them, how are they going to do business with you?

Facebook Business Pages

If you want to pub your business on Facebook, you need a business page. You may or may not need a group to go with it. A business page, is your business's public, outward facing persona. It is not a separate account that you set up for all your business contacts, but rather a page that you create on Facebook. It's managed by your personal page, and whomever you allow to manage the page.

It is important that you go onto your page, and check all the fields regularly, as Facebook will sometimes decide to introduce new features to pages, that can leave you leave you with blank spots on your page.

It's important that you update the following on your page, to get the best results:

1. Your header graphic - should be updated seasonally or more often as appropriate. It can be a graphic or a video, but it needs to be interesting and eye-catching.

2. Your profile picture - you can decide whether you want this profile picture to be your logo, or a professional headshot of you. If you have multiple employees, and are scaling your business, it is probably better to use your logo, otherwise, use a head shot. And, make sure it's professional.

3. About - Fill out the about section completely. Your address, phone number (you can use a Google voice number if you like), description, and other information should be fully filled out.

4. Services or Products - If your business offers products or services, you need to make sure to fill out that section to represent your business well online.

5. Group - If you have a group, you can link it to your business page, and it will be listed under groups for the page.

6. Photos - It almost doesn't matter what your business is, you need to add photos to catch people's eyes.

7. Posts - If you're going to have a business page, you need to post periodically to the page. It doesn't need to be every day, but you should post regularly and/or use the social media platform tools.

8. Stories - Facebook has recently introduced stories, and you can update these to reflect what's going on in your business.

9. The Button - Make sure you update the button on your page to reflect what you'd like for people to do after visiting your page.

Your focus with posts should be to put interesting and engaging posts on your page on a regular basis. This is far easier said than done. Depending on how many people like your page, will depend on how many MIGHT see your posts. You must strike a balance between different types of content if you are a business owner, and that is hard to do.

A Facebook page is your way of sharing information about your business in a public setting. You can build a following, and share events and information about your business. It's mostly intended as a broadcast channel where people are invited in to engage with you, like how your personal page works, but in a less personal, more business-like kind of way.

Ads: A Necessary Evil

Facebook has increasingly become a pay-to-play environment. Organic reach has been dissipating over time. In fact, it's not unusual to see reach on a post be only two or three views. All in all, it's pretty depressing. The days of being able to simply post on your wall and be seen by prospective clients are gone.

Instead, you need to focus on two things: engagement and ads.

Your posts should draw people in and keep them engaged with your business. If you have a particularly fun page, people will seek you out.

Paid ads are a necessary part of any social media strategy. You purchase real Facebook ads for your business. They should represent a part of your ad budget and will bring you benefit.

When I speak of ads, I'm not talking about post boosts. In fact, I generally recommend against boosting posts on your Facebook page, as it does not usually have a strong call to action and doesn't allow for the best possible targeting.

Instead, use real Facebook ads, and post engaging content on your wall for maximum effect.

Facebook Groups

A Facebook group is a community. It can be a community around a common interest, a common cause, or around your business. But at the core it is a community. When I set out to create the Women's Entrepreneur Network, I set out to create a community of women business owners around the globe.

What I learned is that building a group is a very different animal than building a page, and every bit as frustrating in unique and different ways.

Engagement is, and always will be the holy grail of social media. Your page, your account, your groups, everything lives or dies on engagement. If you can't get people to engage with your content, and start to post their own in a group, you are going to be doomed to a group of crickets.

Sure, people may come in, read a post, and then leave, but they're not going to engage.

A lot of people ask me how to grow their group. The simplest and most honest answer is engagement. You can run ads, to get people to find your group, but if there's nothing for them to sink their teeth into when they arrive in the group, they won't hang around, and you will have lost them. Make it so that they WANT to come and hang out with you.

How do you do that? Entertain them, educate them, give them something they crave, and want. Once you've done that, give them something they need.

The way that I did that in the Women's Entrepreneur Network was to ask silly questions like whether toilet paper should be hung over or under. I then followed those silly questions up with more serious questions, and comments. Entertain them educate them, ask them thought provoking questions. Even if you're the expert, let other people show what they know.

Sharing the limelight with others so that you can showcase one another is a challenge, but a necessary one to master if you are going to have a wonderful group. Spotlight others and you'll reap rewards.

Getting the first 100 members into your group

Getting the first 100 members into your group is the hardest part of growing a group. I have seen a lot of people suggest adding all your friends.

DON'T do this!

You'll annoy the ever livin' tar out of people who are constantly being added to groups they didn't ask to be added to. In fact, I had to clean myself out of groups as, at one point, I had been added to well over 500 different groups without my permission. I was super annoyed.

What you do instead is reach out to people who you think would be a good fit for your group and INVITE them to join you. Send them a private message or an email and give them the link to your group. This does two things. People request to join on their own, so they aren't miffed, but truly interested. And, in doing so, you don't hit your limits on how many people you can add to the group before you end up in FB jail. Win-win!

Once you've invited all your friends, and that does NOT mean using the Facebook invite feature, you must take it up a notch in your recruiting efforts. You'll need to grow your group with people outside of your current friends list and doing that will take a few different methods.

I suggest taking a multi-pronged approach to growing your group with the following:

1. Promote it on Twitter, and Instagram. It's counterintuitive, but it works like a charm. I found that my group started growing exponentially when I started promoting it on other platforms. Not believing the results, I actually did something similar with other people's accounts as well and got similar results. This does work!

2. Connect your Facebook group to your Facebook page.

3. Promote your group on all your opt-ins if you have them. I recommend whenever someone opts into your list, that you also invite them to join your group. (And like your business page, too!)

4. Focus on engagement inside the group. Believe it or not, an active group, is one that Facebook recommends. So, it's almost a chicken and egg type of problem. Which came first: the engagement or the growth? The truth is that if you can get a handful of people to start engaging regularly in the group, then you'll be more likely to be found.

Twitter

Twitter has changed significantly in the last year or so. Gone are the days of being able to automatically message everyone who has followed you and reusing content.

Twitter used to be a very loud place with people tweeting dozens to hundreds of times a day, thanks to auto-schedulers, and vast libraries of content. The half-life of a tweet was measured in seconds. Yes, seconds.

Now, you can no-longer reuse content exactly, so this is no longer a problem, but the dynamics of the platform are changing dramatically.

Twitter is instead focusing on engagement, and interaction. They have become much more Facebook-like in that they are showing a set number of people your tweets, and then deciding whether to show more people based on reactions the tweets receive. If you get great engagement and interactions, then you'll get more views. If you get less feedback, then you'll be seen by fewer people.

It is important in Twitter that you post regularly, at least once a day, with some sort of content. You must also retweet other people's content, respond to comments, and be engaged with content, if you choose to fully utilize this platform. The more you engage, the better your results will be.

Things to maximize your Twitter Profile:
1. Tweet regularly. At least once a day.
2. Update your header graphic with something interesting and catchy. The

more interesting and catchy your graphic, the better. You can also have a link to a book, or free download listed on your header graphic.

3. Upload a headshot, or logo to the profile picture.

4. Add a description of what your Twitter page is for, and make sure you include the link to a free download in it.

5. List your city and town.

6. Make sure you list your URL for your business in the account.

7. Feature a pinned tweet at the top of your tweets.

In a nutshell: the more you tweet, the better your results on Twitter.

LinkedIn

LinkedIn is generally thought of as the most "professional" of the social media platforms, and the first platform most people think about using when looking for clients.

It can be a tricky platform to manage and navigate, as it has been undergoing many changes in the last couple of years, with a massive emphasis on selling you their paid subscriptions and ads. I get it, they want to make money, and monetize the vast amounts of data, but it has also made the platform more difficult to use, more difficult to do simple searches. Frankly, it's overall less friendly than it had been in the past.

It is still a very viable platform for many business owners though. It's a little bit funny, because on Facebook, you're likely to get messages from people you barely remember who are desperately trying to sell you their direct sales stuff, but on LinkedIn, you're likely to get messaged by just as many people trying to sell you their latest and greatest marketing tools and hacks, especially—wait for it—how to get clients on LinkedIn.

When you start your LinkedIn Profile, it's important to fill out a full profile, add your full name, job description, and history. Make sure you get everything there, including a neat, professional headshot.

Once you have a great profile filled out, it's important to start asking for recommendations. In general, I recommend asking for three to five recommendations at a minimum for every job you've held, and a bit more for recent work. Continue asking for recommendations from as many people as it seems feasible.

In general, you should reach out to people you find interesting, or are working to network with. Also connect with former co-workers and build the number of people you are connected with on LinkedIn.

LinkedIn Pulse

LinkedIn Pulse is the blog function offered by LinkedIn. When it was first introduced, it offered the opportunity to get in front of dramatically huge numbers of people. Now, LinkedIn has changed course, and is no longer putting quite the same focus on Pulse.

One thing that you can do to reuse content, is to publish articles on Pulse a few weeks after you have published them on your blog. Be sure to include a backlink to articles within your own website blog, to build high quality backlinks.

Instagram

Instagram is a wonderful platform for connecting with lots of people. It is entirely visual, so everything posted is a graphic, or it's a video, which makes it quite different than other platforms in some respects.

Instagram is the platform that also uses the most hashtags.

Focus on posting regularly, up to a couple of times per day. Instagram is one platform where more is definitely not more, so posting 20 times per day would be extremely annoying. Keep it down to at most twice a day, and you're good.

Many Instagram accounts follow trends and style options when posting. So, you see posts arranged in a particular pattern on their wall, and color coordinated, and all beautiful. It's a cool form of artistic expression that really isn't seen on other platforms, in the same way. Of course, other platforms don't necessarily allow you to show all your posts together in a grid, so the same artistry can be impossible to achieve on other platforms.

One of my kids' friends artistically arrays her Instagram posts by color, gently transitioning colors from red to purple to blue to green, and so forth. It is really fun to watch the creativity that can be used with the platform in general.

How often should I post?

A lot of people put a great deal of thought into how often they should post on social media. The answer here is that it depends on the platform, what you have to say, how many followers you have and what kind of engagement you create on your accounts.

In general, the following applies:

Platform	Times per day
Facebook Personal Page	1-2, not more than 5
Facebook Business page	1-2
Facebook Group	3-5
Twitter	1-10 +
Instagram	2-3, not more than 4
LinkedIn	1

Pay attention to how much engagement you're getting when you post, so that you don't flood your networks with tons of posts and get lost in oblivion. Facebook will downgrade you if you post too much and aren't getting engagement on your page.

Hashtags

A lot of people are totally confused by hashtags and how to use them well. They think that there is a lot of magic with using them but understanding them is key to wielding that magic. Used correctly, they can be an asset to your social media efforts.

Hashtags can help your posts get noticed on almost every social media platform, but keep in mind, they are used quite differently on each platform. If you were to post 20 hashtags on LinkedIn, people would think you'd gone off your rocker. You can't post the same hashtags on different platforms.

A hashtag is basically a pound sign or "#" followed by a word or phrase. Twitter, and Instagram are helpful by telling you which ones are trending and which ones people are using. You can mix and match, and create your own for social media posts, so that people can find all your posts.

Hashtags can be silly, or sober, and they can be connected with a cause, event, promotion, or almost any other theme that you want to compile a group of posts.

For instance, you can create one for an event, so when people search for your event, they find every post relating to the event. Let's say you were hosting a health fair and you chose "#PeabodyHealthFair2019." All the vendors could use this hashtag to promote and advertise the fair. Prospective attendees could use the hashtag to find information about the fair. And, during the fair, attendees could use the hashtag to post selfies and vendors could use it to promote day-of promotions or giveaways.

Hashtags can have specific uses, or more broad uses. Sometimes they're just silly. But, you need to use the correct amount for each social media system.

So, exactly how many hashtags should you be using on each platform?

Well, Instagram is the most hashtag friendly platform, and it's usual and customary to put as many hashtags as possible, and that you can think of to get attention. That means putting 20 hashtags on posts, although lately, I've noticed a trend towards fewer hashtags, and more readable content.

Twitter works well with two or three hashtags, as does Facebook, and even LinkedIn. Pinterest, on the other hand really doesn't make use of hashtags, and they are not common on that platform at all.

Look at what others are using to see if it makes sense to go with a current popular hashtag or make your own. Whatever you do, just make sure you're using them.

Pinterest

Which of these social media platforms is not like the others? Yep, it's Pinterest.

Pinterest is less of a social platform, and more of a platform to put yourself out there and be found by pictures, and keywords, a lot like a visual google, with several unrelated ads thrown in just to confuse you.

So, how do you use it?

If you're using Pinterest for business, it's obviously a different game than pinning all the shoes, decor, and recipes that catch your fancy. It's about sharing information that people who would be interested in your business would find fascinating.

For instance, if you are a divorce attorney, it might make sense to post not just your own blog posts, but also articles about managing finances during divorce, as well as articles about counseling, relationships, and so forth.

You want at least 15-20% of the pins to be your own, original content, but you also want to be a good sport, and repin other people's content. By being a good steward of the larger community, and offering value, you are more likely to get your own content repinned.

When you load up a pin on Pinterest, it's important to have good graphics. Your pictures should be quality images. Also, you'll need a well-written description that tells people what to expect when they click on the pin. You also want to be careful to make sure that you include proper keywords, so that people who are searching for a particular topic can find you, repin your content, and follow you.

The more people who repin your content, and add your content to their groups, the better, because that's more people who will go to your website, increasing website traffic, and improving your site's SEO.

In order to be able to get more attention on your blog posts, ideally, you'll create a variety of graphics that go with each blog post so that you can test out to see which graphics catch people's attention for repinning, and getting them to head over to your website.

How often should you post on Pinterest?

In general, you should post on Pinterest as many times a day as you can stand. Some experts advocate pinning 70-100 times per day to get maximum visibility. Obviously you'd have to use a scheduler to do this, and Tailwind is a great tool to do this.

Pinterest Group Boards

Building and joining group boards where more people are likely to see your content is one of the holy grails of Pinterest. Since social media is largely a game of how many people see your content, being on an active group board is an excellent way to get your content in front of more people.

The trick is that you need to follow the individual rules that are associated with each group, and make sure that you are repinning your own content, as well as the content of other people.

If you are looking to join groups, try searching for lists of groups, and emailing the group owner, or messaging them on Pinterest. Don't be surprised if you message a bunch, and never hear back. You may even need to start your own group and invite friends to get a group off the ground.

In general, the more specific your group is, the better it will do, and the more pins it will have. The more pins the group has, and the more people pinning to the group, the better. Activity, engagement, and people interacting with the content is the holy grail of all things social media.

Pinterest Tribes

Pinterest tribes are a cool new feature that has recently been introduced by Tailwind. They are like groups, only better, because they are managed by Tailwind, and the rules of each tribe are clearly posted.

The tribes themselves are administered by Tailwind, and they give you an opportunity to share pins with people in your tribe, and get them repinned, without having to be in a gazillion groups. That means your pinning activity can be more concentrated, and more focused on a few groups and boards, rather than trying to post content in 20 different boards each day.

If you are serious about using Pinterest to grow your business, then get Tailwind. They have a free version you can try out, but you'll need to upgrade to the paid version of it to continue.

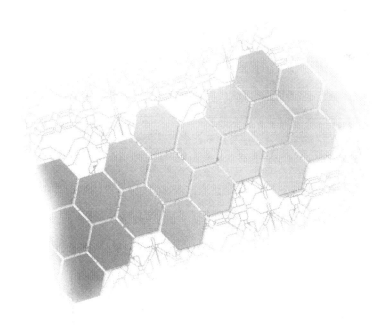

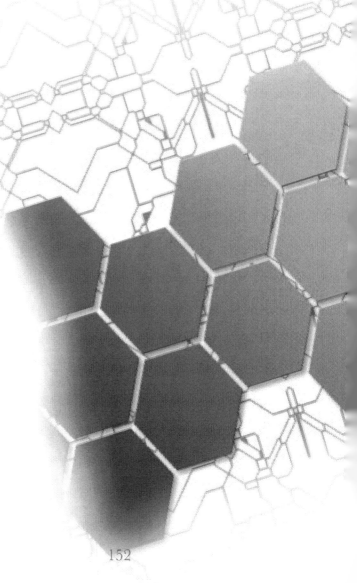

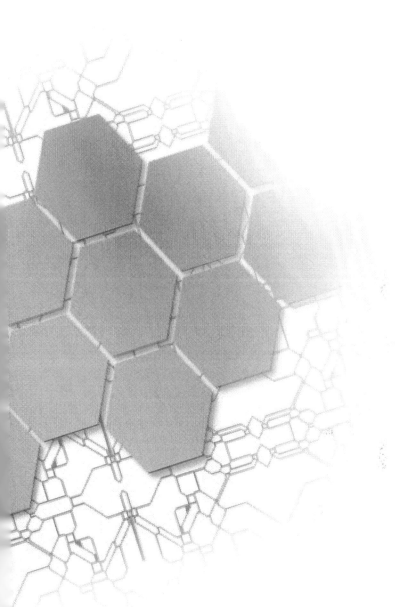

13. The Organic List GrowthModel: Virtual Summits

"Real-time, live
events carry with
them high energy.
Everything happens
live, and it feels more
spontaneous."

13. The Organic List GrowthModel: Virtual Summits

Virtual Summits can be a tremendous way to organically grow your list, and add new, highly targeted prospects to your list who have a high probability of converting.

They can also be a massive time sink, with no return, and a complete waste of your investment, if you aren't careful.

That's why it's important to work with someone who has experience in managing summits if you do decide that you want to do one of your own.

A virtual summit is an online event that can be run several different ways, but the idea is that you bring experts together who are all talking about a narrow range of topics, or they each have a single topic, and share that with your audience.

Talks can either be pre-recorded, or they can be delivered in real time, depending on the number of speakers, time zones involved, and the intent of the organizer.

Real-time, live events carry with them high energy. Everything happens live, and it feels more spontaneous. People feel a part of something that's immediate. The downside is that it takes much more coordination to host a live summit. It takes nearly as much planning as with a location event. Timing and schedules are high considerations.

Pre-recorded summits offer much more flexibility. They can be held as a time-specific summit for the audience, or on an access-at-will basis. For time specific, recorded summits, the audience might have access to the videos for a set amount of time after the summit, for an additional fee, or offered as part of the original ticket.

To participate in a summit, the audience either must sign up and offer up their email address to participate, or they must purchase a ticket to attend.

The idea is that the speakers must help promote the event, and that it's a cross pollination exercise where everyone promotes the event on social media as well as their email list. It can be a wonderful experience for everyone because collective efforts raise much more awareness and attendance.

What are some "must haves" for summits?

Each expert needs to have an active, engaged audience of their own. Without a list, it can be almost impossible for them to effectively bring very many people to the event, which means a lower rate of return for everyone participating.

A. Each expert must actively promote the event. With no promotion, there are no attendees, and with no attendees, it is a flop.

B. The topic must be very narrow. The narrower the topic is, the better.

C. As I learned, it can't just be business, or marketing. It needs to be about a single sub-topic in the range, that will draw a very specific audience.

D. Begin with the end in mind. Decide what you want the attendees of this summit to do afterwards.

E. Plan all your emails in advance, to the attendees, to the speakers, both during, and after the summit.

F. Consider contests to encourage your speakers to participate more fully. The more that your speakers participate, the more your overall participation rate will increase.

G. Consider several ways to monetize the summit. This includes such things as: upselling a VIP pass; creating an e-book from the recordings; selling packages of the recordings; and, the like. The more creative you are with the process and what you do with the information, the better it will work for you.

H. Your copy must be on point. Even if you have everything else, the copy on your website must be perfect. The same is also true for any videos that you release for the event.

In short, it's about planning, strategy, and making sure that you are very careful with your planning so that you get the results you're looking for with a summit. Failure to put all the pieces together will result in a lot of work for approximately zero return, which just is not a happy place to be.

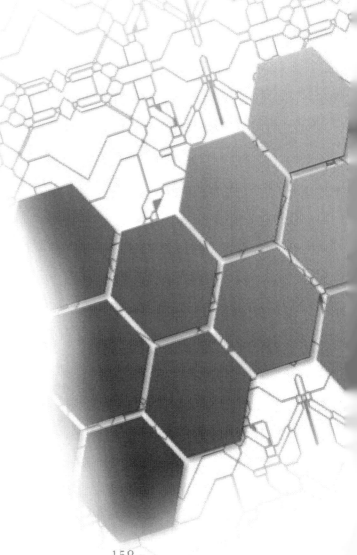

FEAR**LESS** MARKET**ING**

Your 8-Figure Business Blueprint

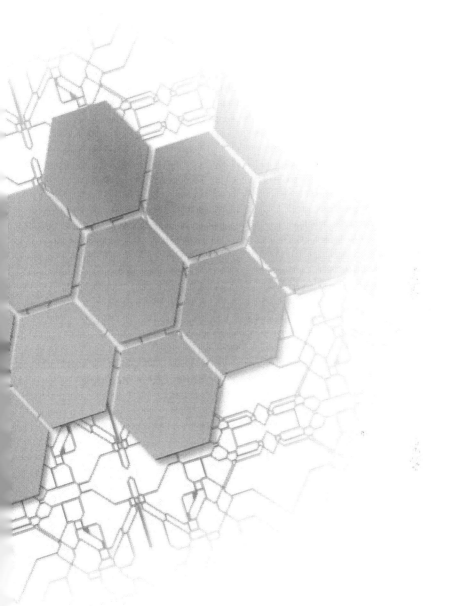

14. It's All About the Raving Fans

"When the rubber
hits the road, it's
about your reputation
in your business."

14. It's All About the Raving Fans
When the rubber hits the road, it's about your reputation in your business that will determine your success or failure.

This is a majorly tricky thing, because there will be some people who love you, and the work you do, and others who really are not that into you. It's important to find the people who are going to be your most ardent supporters and raving fans to choose as your clients.

Not everyone is an ideal client, even if they fit your target demographic. I've run into this a couple of times with website designs. We work very hard to create something that we think the client will love, and nothing we do will make them happy. That's the time to let those clients go. Better to say goodbye and seek to find those people who will be your raving fans, before everyone is miserable.

As a friend of mine said, you want to find your A and B clients, and focus only on those. You may or may not be able to keep your C clients, if you can rehab them. It's time to let those D and F clients go. That really stuck with me. I realized that my D and F clients are the ones who suck up 90-95% of my energy and are never going to be happy. They are also more likely to stiff you when it comes time to pay the bill. (Been there, done that. Always get a down payment.)

My focus then turned to figuring out more about my A and B clients. What do they like? What attracted them to me in the first place? How did I find them in the first place?

Once you have clients, then it is imperative to focus on client satisfaction. Once you have the right clients, every client is precious, and should be treated as such. You can spend your quality time with people who matter to you.

What are the things you need to do to delight your clients? How can you over-deliver? Now, I'm not necessarily talking about throwing in a ton of free services or being available all hours of the day and night, but providing exceptional service, with phenomenal reporting. Answer your phone, texts, or emails in a timely manner. Be present. Be reachable. Be intensely interested in them.

I learned that I don't have to be the best website designer (shhh), but I do have to consistently deliver what I say I'm going to deliver, and make sure that everything is finished...to the client's satisfaction.

It doesn't matter how artistic you are, or how pretty your websites if they are full of errors, and lack half the content that the client requested. If your website just flat out doesn't work, or is never completed, pretty doesn't factor in. People aren't going to be happy if they are missing stuff on their website, and you aren't responsive about getting those errors fixed.

I'm not saying you must be perfect, just that you have to try, and make a point of doing a great job for every client. Once you have an established track record, it is much, much easier to grow your business, and get more clients.

Here are some things that you can do to generate raving fans:

A. Answer your phone. If you can't or won't answer it, then make sure you update your voicemail to reflect that status.

B. Answer your emails. I'm not sure why this is a mystery to people, but make a point of responding to emails within 24-48 hours.

C. Provide regular status updates to your clients. Where it's appropriate, provide regular status. Shipped something? Status. Something changed? Status. Progress? Status!

D. Do what you say you're going to do. I know, I don't know why this is a huge mystery too! But seriously, do what you say you're going to do, when you say you're going to do it!

E. Write thank you notes. Handwritten. Always.

Enter each client engagement with the intent that you will be turning this client into your raving fan. Your work, your efforts, your service and product will all reflect that. And, they will become your most serious, awe-struck, stinking number-one fan.

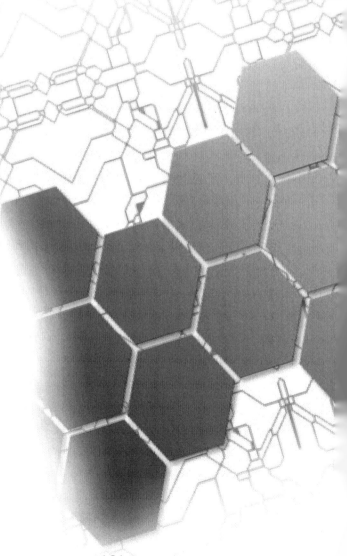

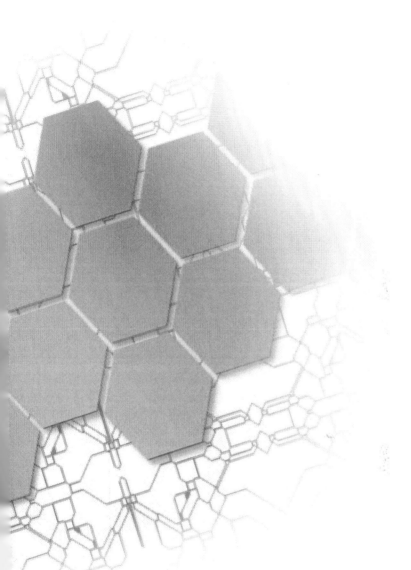

15. The Great Mystery of the Hand Written Thank You Note

"It's far better to send that beautiful, hand-written card, without the business card inside."

15. The Great Mystery of the Hand Written Thank You Note

A few years ago, I was sitting in a friend's office, and I looked around. I noticed that she had various cards posted in her office. They were all hand-written cards. Some were hand-made cards, some were simple thank-you cards. I noticed that the ones she kept were the prettiest ones, because they brightened up her office.

I had always written cards to people in social occasions and had been sending professional cards with the company's logo on the front occasionally, with a nice little note and a business card inside them.

What I realized was that she had a preference (as did most other people I ended up polling) for beautiful, original cards, without a business card inside of them. It's almost as if that business card tainted the rest of the envelope, and the sentiment behind it. People will know who you are, and remember you fondly, even without a business card enclosed. Maybe especially because there's not a business card enclosed.

At a loss for words? Here's some starters…

"You're a joy to work with."
"I'm/We're honored to help your business."
"You knocked my/our socks off!"
"We are all still smiling after your visit."
"You made my/our day."
"Thanks for being you!"

Then, go on to briefly explain HOW and WHY. Keep it short, and keep it neat, but always write from the heart.

It's far better to send that beautiful, hand-written card, without the business card inside, and then follow up by sending a LinkedIn connection request or a Facebook friend request to stay top of mind. The card must stand alone. The social media requests come later.

That way, you'll be top of mind all the time, not just the 30 seconds they spend opening your card. You will stay in front of them, while they keep your beautiful card, and every time you post something interesting and thought provoking on social media.

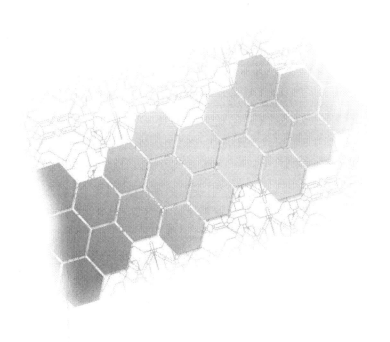

Your 8-Figure Business Blueprint

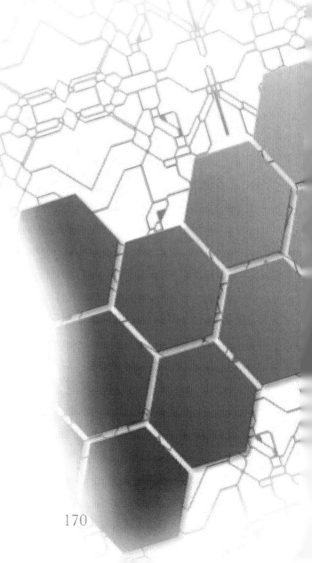

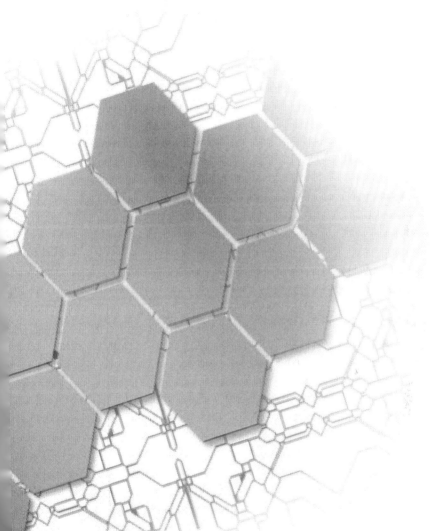

16. Branding, It's Not Just a Logo

"The buck stops
with you.
You are the one
who is going to live
with your schedule
and with
the results of that
schedule."

16. Branding, It's Not Just a Logo

One of THE biggest misconceptions in business is that your brand is your logo. End of story.

I'll give you a hint: it's not. It's also not what you do to cattle to mark them as belonging to your ranch, either. That's what my brother suggested it was. Very helpful brother. Siblings are like that: very funny.

Your brand is really about the way that your business interacts with the world. How does it make people feel? What it the user experience?

Is your brand a Walmart brand? Is it a McDonald's type of brand? Or maybe your brand is more like a Ritz-Carlton, or even a boutique lingerie store?

What kinds of feelings, thoughts, sensations do you want to evoke in your clients and in the public when they meet your brand and your company?

Your brand is encompassed and embedded in your logo, the fonts you use, the colors you use, the language you use, and even the smell of your office. There are fragrance companies that develop signature scents for stores and businesses to convey an atmosphere brand to evoke certain responses.

That is what a good brand does. It evokes a certain set of responses in the client base.

An effective brand helps you stand out from all the rest of the noise. It allows you to distinguish yourself from the thousands of other, similar businesses out there. It's what makes you different, unique, and what makes you appeal to certain buyers.

Think about it. When you go to Walmart, you know what you're going to get. Shelves stocked a certain way, mobs of people, skylights, branded signage, fluorescent lighting, and long lines. The entire feeling of the store is great piles of good stuff cheap, and it's all about rock bottom pricing. Of course, whether the prices really are the lowest, is impossible to predict, but you certainly feel like you're getting a bargain basement experience. No one is going to take your groceries out to the car for you! People of Walmart is a thing. You know that you're going to be joining the masses of humanity when you go to Walmart. You come to expect it, and part of the fun shopping there is wondering what exactly you might run into next.

When you go shopping at Jimmy Choo, it is an entirely different experience. There are a few people in the store, and it is bright and cheery, but not a single harsh, off-colored fluorescent light in sight. The carpet is thick and plush, and people speak in hushed voices. The sales people are all immaculately dressed. The experience is luxurious, the shoes are pristine, and the entire atmosphere is one of complete luxury. You would expect luxury if you're spending $750 on a pair of shoes. Exclusive luxury.

That's the difference in branding. Think about what kind of experience you want to convey to your clients, and what kind of experience you want them to have, and strive to create that ambience, and atmosphere.

If you're still working on your brand, make it a priority as you're out shopping, dining and utilizing businesses, to notice branding. Use all your senses to notice what each business is trying to convey. Or, is it "off?" Are they not pulling it off as a brand? Look for the good flow, and the disjointed alike.

Noticing what works and what doesn't work is helpful for you as you formulate or re-formulate your brand. Not to copy, never to copy another brand, but to see how each brand permeates the store and your experience as customer. Then, translate that to your business. How can you cohesively arrange your logo, font, colors, images, smells, furnishing, fabrics, paint, sounds, music, etc. to reach your audience?

It's not just the logo, but the packaging, the lettering, and the placement of the products that counts. No detail is too small, and no detail should be overlooked.

Do you need to start with a massive brand discovery? No. In most cases, just starting with a consistent look and feel is enough. You can purchase an inexpensive logo from Fiverr, or 99 Designs. Once your business grows a little bit, or a lot, it will be the time to develop your brand further and pay even more attention to things. In the beginning, keep it simple, and go from there.

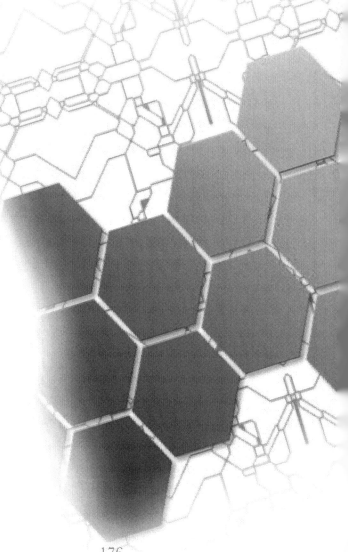

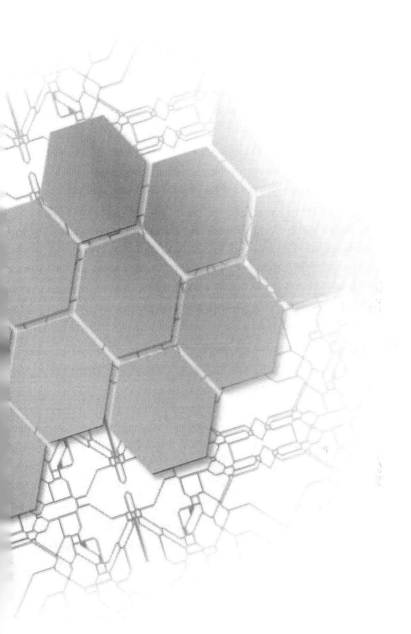

17. The Super Easy Stuff

"When you first
start your business,
there are some
things that you need
to set up."

17. The Super Easy Stuff

When you first start your business, there are some things that you need to set up that are so easy that you should just get them set up, so you can forget about them. They may seem super obvious, but I know that I have gone long periods without making sure that I've taken care of these things.

1. Email Signatures. Make sure that you set up your email signatures on all your devices. That means your computer, laptop, iPad, phone, and any other device you might send email from—as well as signatures for all your email addresses. Your email signature needs to include your name, business name, email, and phone number at a minimum. Once you have a website, it should include your website, and directions for the best ways to get in touch with you.

2. Voice Mail. Make sure you setup your voicemail messages, and set expectations for when people should expect a response from you. If you intend to respond to all voicemails within a certain time period, say so. If you are like me, and suck at checking voicemail messages, set the expectation, and tell people what they should do instead. I ask people to not leave me a message, and to instead hang up, and text me, or email me, so that I get their message in a timely manner.

3. Text Auto Responses. If you work using your cell phone make sure you set up your text auto responses to respond when you're driving, or unable to respond to the phone. Let people know when you will respond and set expectations accordingly. Pretty much every mobile device will allow for a do not disturb option, and you should use this when driving, as well as when you really should not be disturbed.

4. When you set up your social media, make sure you give people a way to find your website, and to get in touch with you. I know that I have gone through phases of making sure that this has been done for my own business, and times where it is not. Take the time to go through all your accounts about once a year or so (or when you go through a major rebrand), and make sure that everything has current contact information. Sometimes things will become out of date, or may not have correct information on them, because entropy just happens.

5. Verify things like Google My Business, Yahoo, Yelp, Bing, etc., at least once every few months. It is totally worth checking up and making sure that all your contact information is listed and correct on all the major directories in addition to all of the major social media platforms at least once a year. Entropy happens in the weirdest places, and sometimes things get updated to reflect old data that you had previously corrected.

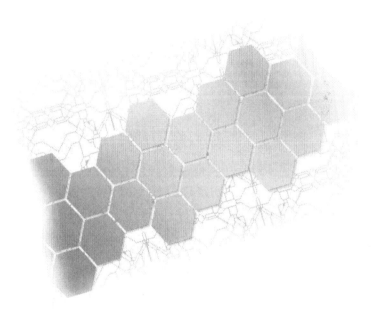

Your 8-Figure Business Blueprint

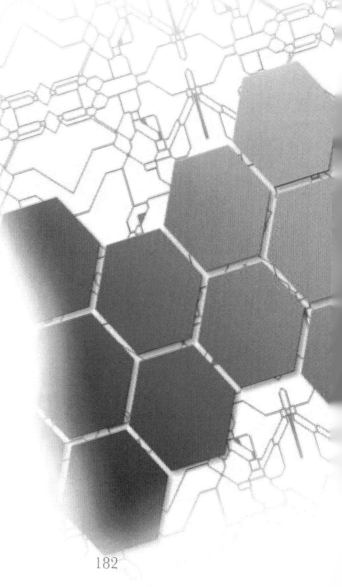

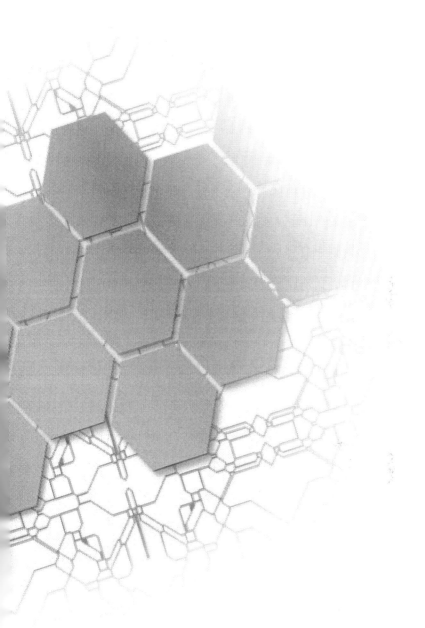

18. Your Action Plan. Just Do It, Now!

"You do not need to
be posting on every
single social media
platform right out
of the gate."

18. Your Action Plan. Just Do It, Now!

What do you do first? How do you decide?

It can seem totally overwhelming to go through a book like this and see all the stuff that I say you should be doing. The good news is that you don't have to do everything all at once. You don't even have to do everything that I've mentioned.

You just need to do something.

The best thing to do is to understand who you are marketing to, and then get the beginning stuff done. Make sure you do things like update your address, phone number, and contact information as appropriate.

You do not need to be posting on every single social media platform right out of the gate. Well, unless your hobby is posting on social media. In which case, knock yourself out. You might not need to post on any social media platforms, depending on the nature of your business, and how people typically find you.

If you try to do everything, you'll drive yourself nuts, and spend all your time marketing, and never get any real work done. That's not a great situation. Obviously, if you don't have many clients yet, you need to do more, rather than less, but it's still about balance.

Figure out who you serve and start marketing to them!

$0 to $350,000/year Level

For those of you in the $0 to $350,000 per year sales range, you will find that you spend most of your time marketing. Once you go above that, it is all about process, and process improvement. If you can spend some time at the beginning of your business figuring out what your processes are, and should be, you will save yourself aggravation and heartbreak when you grow your business to the point of needing to hire others.

In general, the fastest, cheapest way to get clients is to get out and start meeting people. If you have the budget, then focus on Facebook and Google ads in addition to networking. Businesses are built on people and relationships—you remember that know, like, and trust factor? The sooner you can build up that social Karma, the better.

What about Family and Friends?

One of the big secrets in business, that people get extremely upset about—*like seriously heartbroken!*—is that their family and friends don't support their business.

I can't tell you how many stories I've heard about people who say that their own sister would rather go to the shop down the street than buy from them. In fact, I've heard it said that their relatives actively avoid doing any kind of business whatsoever with them, and it breaks their heart.

Hurt feelings are a huge deal here, and I want to say that I totally understand. My husband is not supportive of my business at all, unless it's making a lot of money. In many cases, he's actively resented it. My sister-in-law has asked me numerous times if the business is so much work, why don't I just give up and go get a real job.

It stings, and it hurts. Some family members will understand, and some will never get it. It's important to forgo expectations altogether. Do not expect all your family members to buy from you, or to have them even support your business.

You can expect that some of them will think you're totally ridiculous for posting about your business on social media and may even try to shame you into not posting. You must ignore them. You must let it go. Go work on your business and go work on getting clients. Ignore the nay-sayers, haters and sticks-in-the-mud. Your job is to make your business work, and only you can do it.

If you are one of the lucky ones who has a family who supports them in

usiness, be glad. Be very glad, and very grateful, for you have been truly bless-
. Let them know it, too!

300,000-$1,000,000 Level

nce you get to $300,000-$1,000,000 sales per year range, you might be think-
g things are going great, until they just start to unravel and fall apart in strange
ays, pushing you back down. You start to think you've arrived, and suddenly,
e gremlins start to show up in your business, and push you back down.

arketing, and marketing process becomes imperative at this point, if you don't
ready have it in place. You will likely also find that you need to take a step
ack, and analyze your end-to-end client process, as well as add new ways of
tting clients.

ocess may not sound sexy, but it will literally save your hiney in business. It
n make or great your business, and save you as you add employees, and start
really grow your revenues.

ur Checklist
  • Analyze Your End-to-End Process
  • Refine Your Customer Pipeline: Sales Funnel
  • Upsells and Cross Sells
  • Scripts
  • Radio, TV, Live Videos, YouTube Channels, and Podcasts…Oh My!
  • Hiring Your First Sales Development Staff

et's review each of these to get you going.

nalyzing Your End-to-End Process

ur end-to-end client experience is going to be critical to make sure that you
e maximizing your revenues and continuing to grow your business.

you don't have sales funnels, follow up processes, scripts for answering the
one, and an upsell process, then now is the time to develop those.

u are also going to want to start growing where you get leads from, and that
ely is going to include things like books, Radio, TV, and paid ads.

Refine Your Customer Pipeline: Sales Funnel

Automated sales funnels are a great way to follow up when you can't. Many times, I see them used heavily in the online space, but they are crazy good in the offline space.

For instance, if you are an attorney, who wants to automatically follow up with prospects who have had a consultation, but who have not paid a deposit, then a simple follow up sequence makes sense. Add in some extra automation like texts, or knowing when someone has opened an email, and you can automatically follow up with clients, and remind your staff to follow up with them as well.

Or imagine another scenario- in North Carolina, a Divorce requires a year of separation. You could automatically set your system up to follow up with clients just before and after that 1 year mark. You could also schedule reminders for these clients to re-evaluate child custody agreements, child support, and to update their wills. All important pieces of information for a client who has gone through a divorce, but not necessarily something that you will remember to do by yourself.

These types of funnels and sequences bring more business in the door by helping prospects build that lovely know, like, and trust factor, as well as staying in front of them- all without having to remember, track it on spreadsheets, and take tons of valuable time away from you or your team.

What Exactly *IS* a Sales Funnel?

A sales funnel is the process that you follow in your business to take people from "out there in the ether sphere" to being one of your clients.

I'm referring to using an automated sales funnel for this process. This can be one of the most important investments you make in your business, as it can help reduce labor costs, once it is implemented, save many, many hours of time, and increase your revenues.

Any time you have an ad campaign, or you have a client who has purchased from you before, you want them to buy, or buy again, with as little investment on your side as possible.

A sales funnel can be implemented any of several ways.

1. Webinar: This includes running ads to get people into a call or a webinar. From there, they purchase a product or service.

2. Free Offer. You offer something for free, like a report, or a guide, and people download it. They are then sent into your sales funnel, which includes emails, and upsells. Depending on someone's actions, you use conditional formatting to send them where you want them to go.

3. Follow-up Sequence. This includes a series of emails, texts, etc., that allow you to follow up with a client. It can also involve reminders to you or your team to follow up with the prospect, in addition to sending them information.

Upsells and Cross Sells

I'm totally guilty of selling someone something, then forgetting to sell them anything else. I mean, they bought, I should be happy, right? That leaves a lot of money on the table.

One of the best upsells I've ever seen came at a Girl Scout cookie booth with my younger daughter, Xena. Someone came up and asked for a box of Thin Mints. She held up a case of Thin Mints, which contained 12 boxes, and a regular box, and asked if they wanted the little box or the big box.

You might not be surprised to hear that she sold many, many cases of Thin Mints (and other flavors of cookies too), just by offering the option.

If you don't give people the option, they won't know they have it. Too often in business we assume that the client or customer knows everything we have, or that they're going to ask for what they want. That means leaving a lot of money on the table.

Think about it this way. It used to be that you would go to McDonald's and buy each item individually. You'd buy the hamburger, the drink, and the fries, separately. The people who did the best at sales knew to ask the customer if they'd like fries with their order.

The company eventually caught on and started offering bundles of products, now called meals, and numbered them. Now, you go to any fast food restaurant, and can either order by number or by name.

That gives those companies the opportunity to then cross sell you a dessert, or to sell you the large size of the combo. Those things dramatically increase sales and improve the bottom line.

List all your products and services. What items naturally go together? Where are there gaps that you can additional items?

It almost doesn't matter what your business is, there are opportunities for upsells, and bundles. If you aren't looking for them in your business, you are missing out.

Scripts

As you scale your business, scripts are going to become a MUST HAVE for marketing and sales.

When someone answers your phone, do you know what they're saying, and how they're saying it?

Do you know for sure that the person answering is getting all the appropriate information, or selling the right things to the callers?

These things can all be improved with checklists and scripts.

One of my chiropractor clients put a mirror in front of his receptionist under the counter but at face-height for his staff. Why? Because people can "hear" a smile over the phone. Did you know that? Yes, people can hear smiles over the phone. If they can hear smiles, they can hear frowns, too. So, what's with the mirror? Well, if someone looks in the mirror, they tend to smile. By having that mirror at the reception desk, his receptionist smiled more while on the phone, and gave a better sounding voice when talking to clients.

Have you ever called a business and had a terse receptionist speak to you in monotone and/or unfriendly voice? Maybe she's a lovely person, but she comes across like you are wasting her time. This is completely unacceptable for any business. As the owner, you must ensure that your staff are pleasant and friendly with your clients, and they know what you want them to say.

For that, you'll need to write out scripts. Not for them to read, but so they know what they should be saying. Many times, what they should say seems obvious, but it's not always apparent to them. You need to have a McDonald's attitude toward answering the phone—it should be identically answered every single time.

You must also plan for contingencies with good training and more scripts. Nothing is more annoying than calling into a business and the person who answers the phone doesn't know anything. They keep putting you on hold to have questions answered. You don't have time for that, and neither do your clients. It has the added detriment that it makes you look incompetent. Your staff is an extension of you, so have them well-trained and well-scripted.

But, you say, I don't have a staff, this doesn't apply to me. Yes, it does. Make a script, even for yourself. You'll speak differently on different days depending on your mood. You don't want your mood to determine your client interactions. We all have good days, better days and bad days. Write scripts for you. And, when you grow, you'll have a staff that you can train to do the same.

What do scripts have to do with Marketing? Well, I maintain that the sales and marketing process should be seamless from end-to-end. Thus, you need to make sure that you are setting up your processes, so that the person who is calling in, replying to an ad, receives the correct response from you and your team.

Your messaging and responses need to match across the board, and reflect your brand and image, regardless of the mode of communication. You do this with scripts and training.

Radio, TV, Live Videos, YouTube Channels, and Podcasts...*Oh My!*

To reach more people in your business, you might want to eventually try video, tv, radio, or podcasts to build up even more of an audience.

Say, you are a brick and mortar business, like an attorney or chiropractor, and not a coach. These methods of marketing your business can still be very helpful, believe it or not. For people to want to buy from you, as I can't stress enough, they must know, like, and trust you. Video and audio are a great way for people to interact with your brand and get to know you over time. That way, they feel like they can trust you, even if you haven't directly interacted with them.

This can be part of the secret sauce for scaling your business.

You can leverage these platforms together and distribute various components via different channels to get far more bang for your buck.

Imagine for a second that you record a video, or tv interview. That can be uploaded to YouTube, and your YouTube channel. It can also be embedded in to your website for additional content.

Many times, it's also possible to have a separate audio recording of a TV show, or video. It can become a podcast, with only a little bit of production magic.

Take the audio, for instance, and have it transcribed. Now, you have an eBook, or the fodder for several blog posts and articles. You can then either post these to your own blog, or you can submit them to other websites for publication. You can also choose to publish the entire transcript, audio, and video together on your website, to give your audience a multi-sensory experience.

Take some key soundbites out of the recordings, and turn them into a variety of graphics, using pre-created templates. You can use Canva or a similar photo editor to create those graphics for a strong visual reminder of the article, then use them on your website, social media, and as Pinterest pins to send traffic back to your website.

It's a strategy of content creation, and use and reuse, that can stretch for miles. All from a single video, or interview.

How do you get a Podcast?

So, if having a podcast or radio show is so great, then how do you get one? In short, it's super easy to record a podcast and video using software like Zoom, which is free, or low cost, depending on how long your recordings are.

You then work with a company to produce the Podcast, or do it yourself, and upload it to iTunes and other podcast repositories. You put it out there.

Finally, you share the information on your website, as well as your social media, to build your audience, and your expert level status of your business.

Many different types of business owners have turned to this as a very affordable way to get more visibility for your business.

You might be wondering if you should be doing a live Radio show. The answer to that is that it depends on the reach and the cost of producing your show. It can be either very affordable or extremely expensive depending on which options and on which stations you choose to appear. You will get varying mileage out of different providers.

Make sure that no matter what you end up deciding to do, you research your options carefully.

Guest Blogging & Guest Podcasting

Say that you like to write but aren't too sure you want to write on a regular basis. Or that you are trying to build up an audience and get more people to find you to learn about your business.

A good step into the blogging and podcasting arena is to be a guest. You can appear on as many podcasts and submit as many articles to other sites as you desire. You can do these on your timetable as determined by your energy level. These guest appearances will help you find new audiences and get seen and heard by more people.

Afterall, the bigger your audience, the more likely you are to find your ideal clients. Working with a company that provides PR or booking services can be a wonderful investment in your business to help you grow.

Another cool thing is that you can share the same message repeatedly, and not have to develop 20 or 30 different topics to present. It will save you time in development of your various subject matter for speaking.

Leveraging other people's audiences gives you a great opportunity to get seen and heard. You and your business are placed directly in front of a pool of potential clients, none who have heard of you before.

Hiring your First Sales Development Staff

As your business grows, at some point, you will need to hire your first sales and marketing staff. The challenge is making sure that you have the job well defined. That way, they can do a great job for you, as well as ensuring you have the capacity to handle the volume of business being generated by that person.

With any position, there are a lot of unknowns. When you hire someone who is doing business development or sales, you are potentially hiring someone who can be your biggest revenue generator, or your biggest bust.

You want to make sure that you are measuring their activities, and especially their results, so that you know what you're getting out of the deal.

Here are only some questions to answer, and there are more:

How many calls/appointments are they expected to make per day/per week?
- How many accounts do they contact and how many do they service?
- Do they go to networking meetings and other events on your behalf?
- How do you document their activities--CRM?
- Do you track their location on a phone?

I've had friends' businesses get into real trouble with salespeople because the terms weren't written down and enforced. It's not enough to spell out how your salesperson spends their time, you must monitor, as well as enforce the agreed upon job requirements. Have termination plans in place before you hire. It sounds disheartening, but sometimes it takes going through a few different salespeople to find your perfect match.

Hiring a sales person can be one of the best investments in your business, but you must verify, and make sure that you're getting what you're paying for. Oversight is the key to sales staff management, as well as clearly defining their goals and consequences for not meeting them.

Why Social Media and Your Salespeople Don't Mix

It will probably be incredibly tempting to have your sales people be responsible for social media in a small business. Or to have someone in your office just "do" the social media. Unless they are good at managing social media, and very effective with their use of time, this can be a spectacular waste.

Don't be fooled into thinking that just because someone is good at posting on social media, that they will be good at sales, or because they are good at sales, they should be doing social media. This is a huge trap that I fell into with my first business, and I've seen other small business owners fall into it as well.

You'll want to have salespeople doing sales and hire a social media expert to do you your social media. The two are completely different skill sets.

Generally, good sales people will stay so busy that they don't really have the time to manage social media, and it will get neglected. They may also not have the skills to manage ad campaigns, so they will end up boosting posts, and wasting money. It frequently ends up not being a good scenario on any level. Just avoid it.

$1,000,000 + Level

When your revenues hit $1,000,000 and up, your marketing becomes about scaling and processes.

If you don't already have a plan in place to audit your business processes, now is the time to get it in place. Ideally, audits should happen at least once a year. Just as you would audit finances, it's time to examine your processes, for things like bottlenecks, breakdowns in communication, and places where you find that you're spending too much money.

At this point, you're hiring employees, and those employees need to understand what your marketing campaigns are, what you're selling, and generally a bit about the business, but they won't understand everything. Each person should have their own specific niche and be focused on delivering services, or products. That makes it both easier and harder to have effective marketing.

Why? Because humans are interesting creatures.

Take the behavioral study of monkeys. There was one study where the monkeys were placed in a cage with a ladder which had a bunch of bananas at the top of it. Obviously, this was a very enticing bunch of bananas, and monkeys being monkeys, they would naturally try to climb that ladder to grab those delicious bananas. When they would start to climb it, out would come the water hose, and everyone would get hosed down, not just the monkey on the ladder.

This trained the monkeys that if you tried to go up the ladder, you were going to get hosed. Something bad was going to happen. Thus, they learned, to NOT go up that ladder, and if anyone tried, they would quickly pull them down, before they got hosed.

Once that phase of the training was complete, the scientists swapped out one of the existing group for another monkey. The new monkey would see that beautiful bunch of bananas at the top of the ladder and try to climb the ladder. The other members of the group would quickly pull the newcomer down, and punish them for attempting to climb the ladder, so that they would understand that climbing the ladder was forbidden.

Then the researchers would swap out yet another monkey. And the training would continue.

This went on until all the original group were replaced with new monkeys. None of them had ever been hosed down, nor did they know why they were not able to go up that ladder, but you can bet that any newcomers were prevented from going up that ladder to get the bunch of bananas.

The researchers no longer needed to hose anyone down, after the first few times, and certainly none of the current members of the group had ever been hosed. They simply followed the rule of "do not climb the ladder."

Humans behave much the same way, and similar cultural patterns will likely start to develop in your own business.

I've experienced it myself in my own business, when we moved to answering the phones 24/7. There were some odd scheduling issues that happened, because of the way that people handled the situation, resulting in extreme increased cost for me, that could have easily been avoided.

If you take the time to audit and understand what your processes are, and WHY you are following them, then you will save money, and become more efficient in your business. You don't want to be doing things in your business just because you've always done it that way. Critically look at what you're doing, to see if change is needed.

Coordinating Marketing, Sales, and Operations Teams

At this point in your business, you may have dedicated sales people, and a separate marketing team. It is important to make sure that everyone is on the same page.

Too often it seems that people would rather die than think. Communication is a close second. As you build teams of people, you will notice the tendency to silo, and to separate different job functions from one another. Sometimes, that goes as far as possible. People can take it to the far side of ridiculous. Liken it to the standard line: "That's not my job."

It would probably be hysterically funny if it weren't so expensive or so serious. I'm convinced that this is a lot of where the material for Dilbert came from. It's funny until it's your own personal finances, and well-being that are affected.

When you have dedicated sales people, it is vitally important to coordinate their messaging with the marketing team, and to make sure that they coordinate with the operations team. It's important to know what is being said to the clients, and what the current message is.

Imagine for instance that you have a special on your website. It is important that the office staff knows exactly what that special is, so when a client calls in to purchase or inquire, they can get the information or appointment they are asking for.

Have you ever had that time when you've called in, with a coupon, or with a special that was being offered, that no-one in the office seemed to know about? Don't let that be you. Or your business.

Instead, what you need to do is have a marketing plan, month by month that is scheduled out months in advance and communicated to your entire team. Everyone.

When you have a schedule, and can plan around it, and market around it, then it becomes dramatically easier to stay in sync with everyone in your business.

To have a successful business, everyone must be on the same page. Schedule regular full staff meetings to disseminate information. Don't rely on group emails or memos; we all know no one reads those. Get everyone together to talk about current promotions, basic offerings, systems and procedures, and, importantly, vision.

Have your Mission Statement and Vision Statement clearly written out and update them if needed, but not often. In fact, well-defined and crafted Mission and Vision statements should last years, decades, or even the life of your business. Your staff should know them by heart. Post them and speak them often. They should be at the heart of everything done in your business.

Hope Community Church here in Raleigh speaks their Mission and Vision statements so frequently that most of the congregation knows them by heart. Vision Statement: "Reach the Triangle; Change the World." Mission Statement: "Love people where they are and help them grown in their relationship with Jesus Christ." Simple, yet complex, but to the point. Everything done in the church, by the church, and by the attenders of the church stem from those statements. If it doesn't, it isn't done.

Do your employees know your Mission and Vision statements by heart? Do they know the core values of your company? Do they know for what you stand? Do they understand why you do what you do? It must be more than just "make money." That is not enough to keep interest. You must have a foundational cause for being in business.

Vision casting must be executed flawlessly at this level of business. You should not be in the $1,000,000 + playing field without definite and precise tenets.

Conclusion
Wrapping it all up and tying it with a bow.

Building a business can seem overwhelming, scary, and frightening. Getting started is the hardest part. Once you start seeing clients, and money starts rolling in, it becomes marginally easier. As my small business owner friend used to tell me, "More sales forgives more sins."

While we never want sales to mask problems in our processes, sales will help smooth over some rough patches as you learn to apply the marketing strategies I've laid out for you. There will be learning curves, and bumps along the way. You may find that what worked last year, isn't doing it for you this year. That's okay. You need to keep sticking with the basics and tweaking them for your business.

Remember, if you don't get the foundation pieces in place, it will be harder to scale your business as you grow, and tougher to make course corrections. Make sure that you have your foundations in place, and running well, before you proceed to more complicated maneuvers. So, start with, or reassess your foundations.

Here is a recap of your marketing blueprint:

CLIENTS: Describe your ideal client and take some time and think about who it is that you serve. You can sell your products or services to a vacuum. You must sell to a person.

ANALYSIS: Analyze your business from end-to-end to figure out where you have missed opportunities for getting repeat business and go grab it: upsell, cross sell and downsell.

MARKETING PROCESSES: To grow your business successfully, you're going to need to start putting marketing processes in place early on in your business and keep tweaking them as you scale.

EVALUATE: Decide which things are the most important to you and decide if the loss of clients for things is okay. Prioritize your life in such a way that you account for the balls that are going to be dropped and let that not cause you stress.

LEADERSHIP: Establishing your leadership early on in your business is going to be super important. You want to make sure that people know you are the go-to expert at what you do.

AUTHOR: Write a book and use it to teach your clients, and as your $5 calling card.

CONNECTOR: If you want to more clients, become someone that gives back. Be the go-to connector.

WEBSITE: A good website can help you get more clients because people are more likely to be able to find you online.

SALES FUNNEL: You want to have people become aware of your business and products by following a specific set of steps on the way to becoming a client.

SEO: Search Engine Optimization drives more traffic to your website and bring more eyeballs to your products or services.

ADVERTISING: Targeting is the most critical part of understanding and predicting whether ads will work in the first place.

SOCIAL MEDIA: Choose a platform you like, and one you can maintain initially, before calling in a professional. Once you've had some success, you can then afford to hire someone to do it on your behalf.

SUMMITS: Virtual Summits can be a tremendous way to organically grow your list, and add new, highly targeted prospects to your list who have a high probability of converting.

RAVING FANS: Your reputation in your business determines your success or failure. It's important to find the people who are going to be your most ardent supporters and raving fans to choose as your clients.

THANK YOU NOTE: Send a beautiful, hand-written card, without the business card inside, and then follow up by sending a LinkedIn connection request or a Facebook friend request to stay connected.

BRANDING: Your brand is encompassed and embedded in your logo, the fonts you use, the colors you use, the language you use, etc., with a cohesive, coordinate theme.

SUPER EASY STUFF: The easy stuff, like email signatures, are some things that you need to spend some time setting up so you can forget about them.

ACTION PLAN: You don't have to do everything all at once. You don't even have to do everything that I've mentioned. *You just need to do something. Now.*

Figure out which marketing activities you enjoy, which ones you can hire out, and don't worry about the rest. Just do enough to bring in clients, and you will be set.

As one of my coaches says, "Do the common things uncommonly well!" That means if you send out a newsletter, you send it out regularly, like clockwork. If you post on social media, you do that regularly like clockwork, and post the most beautiful things. Get creative with it. Whatever you do, do it well and consistently.

In the end your business, is yours. Shocker, right? There are very few "right" or "wrong" answers. There are very few things you must do, except pay taxes.

It's not about doing what others tell you to do, but for you to put processes in place that bring you clients and sales. Then, follow those systems to the best of your ability.

To your massive success!

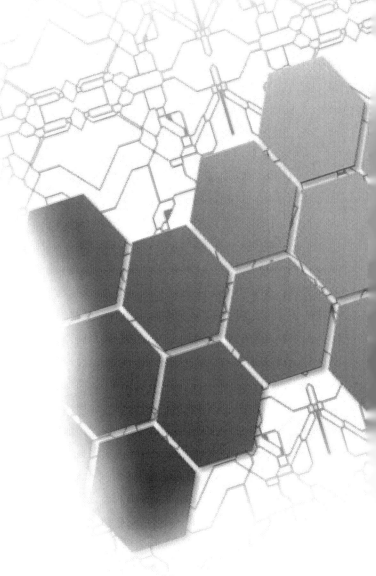

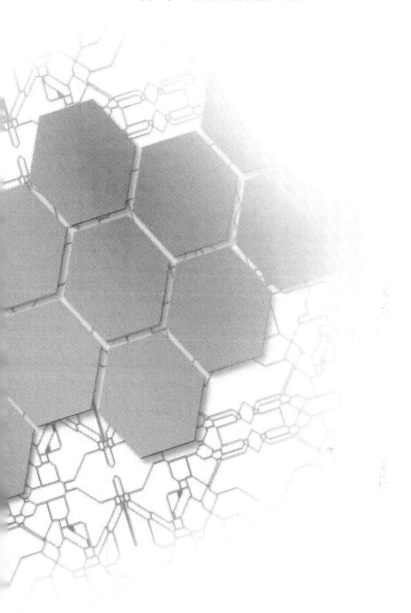

About the Author

Haley Lynn Gray
founded Leadership Girl
Business Coaching, Speaker, Author,
Info@LeadershipGirl.com | (919) 630-2146

facebook.com/leadershipgirl
twitter.com/darthastewart
Linkedin.com/in/haleygray
instagram.com/darthastewart

**Haley Lynn Gray as seen on
ABC, NBC, FOX and CBS**

About the Author

Haley Lynn Gray founded Leadership Girl with the radical notion that women can harness their unique power and skills to become highly effective leaders.

She is the best-selling author of Leadership Girl , and a graduate of Duke's Fuqua School of Business with an MBA with a concentration in entrepreneurship and Innovation. She has experience with starting up successful small businesses, growing them, then selling them.

Headshot of Haley Lynn GrayHaley has worked with hundreds of small business owners since Leadership Girl was founded. She has a passion for helping their owners find ways to grow their business, acquire visibility, and transform into the go-to expert in their industry, while saving them significant amounts of money.

Haley is the founder of the 60,000 strong Women's Entrepreneur Network Group on Facebook, which she successfully grew in only two years. It is recognized as one of the best, most engaging, and helpful groups of this type on Facebook.

By working with clients 1:1, in small groups, and in a variety of different programs, Haley helps clients grow their businesses in a way that makes sense for them, since no two businesses are exactly the same.

It is the belief that each business has its own unique fingerprint. When we recognize and work with each business's unique strengths and weaknesses, then we see the best results.

There is no one size fits all for leadership or business modeling. We are all unique, so playing to our strengths yields the best outcomes.

When Haley isn't working, she is an avid volunteer, and is on the board of directors for Cure AHC, and My Sahana. She is a long-time Girl Scout Troop leader and volunteer.

She is the mother of four active kids, and has a mini zoo in her home, with a variety of pets including cats, a horse, chinchilla, rabbit, fish, and turtles! She understands that sometimes life gets in the way and is messy, but that it is beautiful anyway.

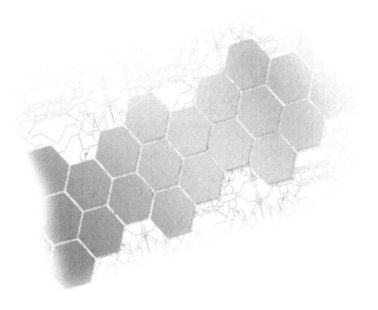

Thank You!

I want to extend a thank you to all of my clients, and my friends who have given me great case studies, information, and an almost indescribable amount of support while writing this book.

Irene Pro. Thank you for being there for me at all hours of the day and night. Thank you for your patience as we have brought this book into existence. I appreciate your kind words, and all that you do for me.

Leslie Flowers. I thank you for cheering me on, and your amazing mastermind. IN it, I have grown my business, while having an almost unimaginable amount of chaos in my life.

Leigh Scheidell. Thank you for the mental health status checks. The last few months have been quite a ride. Having a loved one with mental illness while trying to manage your own life is no joke.

Heather Fein. Thank you for your kindness and great perspective.

ZofiaRenea Morales. Thank you for proofing the book, and giving me such great feedback to make this book better.

Cat Schmidt Lewis. Thank you for editing this book, and helping me make it the way it SHOULD be!

My Family. Thank you for your patience as I've stayed up late nights, and long hours to make this book a reality.

Haley Lynn Gray

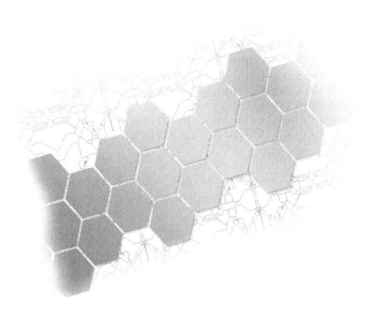